# Professional Obsolescence

A symposium held at Cambridge, England, in June, 1970
Sponsored by the NATO Scientific Affairs Division

Edited by S. S. DUBIN
The Pennsylvania State University

**Lexington Books**
D.C. Heath and Company
Lexington, Massachusetts
Toronto          London

This volume is respectfully dedicated to the late Lord Jackson or Burnley whose spirit and support were so generously extended to us during the planning of the symposium.

Published in the United States of America by Lexington Books, D.C. Heath and Company, Lexington, Massachusetts.

Published simultaneously in Canada.

International Standard Book Number: 0-669-82925-0.

Library of Congress Catalog Card Number: 72-76025.

# Foreword

A symposium on combatting professional obsolescence was held at Churchill College, Cambridge, June 22-26, 1970, under the auspices of the Scientific Affairs Division of the North Atlantic Treaty Organization (NATO). This book is a record of the papers presented at the meetings.

The purpose of the symposium was to bring together persons working in widely scattered locations in Europe and America who were particularly concerned with the subject of professional and technical obsolescence, to provide a situation for the exchange of views, for the presentation of new research and other forms of exploratory and experimental activity; and to make recommendations for further research or programs on the part of the participating nations.

Among the speakers and delegates there were a number of persons of high-level responsibility in their respective organizations or professions. The nations represented were: Belgium, Canada, Federal Republic of Germany, France, Italy, the Netherlands, Norway, Sweden, Turkey, United Kingdom, and the United States. By occupational category, the largest number of individuals came from the universities or from governmental and military offices. In addition, there were representatives from educational administration, management, labour, medicine, and research organizations.

It would be by no means safe to assume that, since the topic of the conference was professional obsolescence, there was unanimity among the participants as to the meaning of that phrase. Indeed, there was much lively argument about the definition of the word *obsolescence*, and widely diverse opinion concerning its origins and contributing factors, the remedies which would be most effective, and the apportionment of responsibility for combatting obsolescence between the individual, the private organization and public sector. Furthermore, diversity of viewpoint was enhanced by the international character of the body of delegates, each of whom contributed a unique insight from his cultural background. If there was any consensus it was that the problem of obsolescence was of great magnitude and immediacy, and that it demanded continuing research, experimental pilot projects, and innovative approaches in order to meet present and future needs.

The editor would like to thank warmly and gratefully Dr. L. Ter-Davtian, of the Office of European Cooperation and Development (OECD) for his finesse in the role of co-director of the conference, and especially for his success in rounding up a number of contributors on the Continent. Finally, there remains for the editor to thank the Scientific Affairs Division of NATO for its financial support and assistance in structuring the conference.

SAMUEL S. DUBIN
Symposium Director

# Contents

**The Magnitude of Occupational Obsolescence
in Engineering and Sciences**
*Lord Jackson of Burnley*
Imperial College of Science and Technology, London.                    1


**Professional Updating for the Advancement
of National Purpose: An Analysis of
U.S. Government Activities**
*Carl York*
Office of Science and Technology
Executive Office of the President, Washington, D.C.                    13


**La Formation en Cours de Carrière dans le Cadre des Travaux
de l'OCDE  (Current OECD Studies on In-Career Education of
Highly Qualified Manpower)**
*L. Ter-Davtian*
Industry and Education Relations, OECD, Paris.                    18


**Motivational Factors in Professional Updating**
*Samuel S. Dubin*
The Pennsylvania State University                    35


**Obsolescence as a Problem of Personal Initiative**
*William R. Dill*
Graduate School of Business  Administration
New York University                    49


**Combatting Obsolescence Using Perceived
Discrepancies in Job Expectations of Research
Managers and Scientists**
*Gerald V. Barrett, Bernard M. Bass and John A. Miller*
Management Research Center
University of Rochester, U.S.A.                    59


**Mid-Career Education:
Its Shape as a Function of Human
Disequilibrium**
*R. M. Belbin*
Industrial Training Research Unit
University College, London                    72

**La Lutte Contre l'Obsolescence chez
les Cadres Promus (Combatting Obsolescence
in Promoted Managers)**
*R. Bosquet*
Enterprise et Personnel
Institut d'Etudes et Developpement
Paris.                                                                          79

**Updating in the Royal Air Forces Training**
*Gilbert Jessup*
RAF, Ministry of Defence, London.                                               86

**Updating Management Practices in Italy**
*G. Martinoli*
Italian National Council of Research, Milan                                     97

**Factors in the Organization Climate
Which Stimulate Innovation in Professional
Knowledge and Skills**
*P. Hesseling*
Netherlands Economics University, Rotterdam
and Philips Company, Eindhoven.                                                 107

**Work and Its Satisfactions in a Technological
Era: A Projected NATO Environmental Study**
*N. A. B. Wilson*
Formerly Chairman, NATO Advisory Group on Human Factors, London                119

# The Magnitude of Occupational Obsolescence in Engineering and Sciences *

Lord Jackson of Burnley    Imperial College of Science
and Technology, London

It does not fall to me to present and argue the need for the continuous in-career updating of the men and women who qualified, at various levels, in one or other branch of engineering or science in their early twenties and who then joined the active stock of practitioners in these fields, though I can hardly avoid dealing with this matter to some extent. I have been asked to try to quantify this need. Clearly this is possible only in general terms, even for my own country; and even if I could do it for the United Kingdom the detailed picture would no doubt differ from that relevant to other countries. Fortunately, great detail and precision are not necessary to recognition of three facts; first, that all countries are faced with broadly the same need and the same associated problems; second, that the need is already large, and is growing larger; and third, that the provisions in further education and training required to resolve it are going to raise considerable organisation and financial difficulties and demand a much closer collaboration between the domains of education and employment than many, if not all, countries have yet achieved. This paper is concerned with portraying the situation within the United Kingdom in the hope that this will encourage the participants from other countries to provide related information, particularly about the steps that have been taken, or are contemplated, to deal with the problems involved.

## THE GROWTH IN ANNUAL UNITED KINGDOM OUTPUT OF GRADUATE ENGINEERS, TECHNOLOGISTS AND SCIENTISTS, AND OF THEIR SUPPORTING STAFFS, OVER THE PAST FIFTY YEARS

Figure 1 shows separately the growths in annual output of graduate engineers and technologists from the Universities and Colleges of Technology; of successful Higher National Diploma and Certificate, and Higher Technician Certificate, candidates from the Colleges of Technology and the Technical Colleges; and of successes in the Technical College courses and examination leading to Ordinary National Diploma and Certificate, and Technician Certificate, awards. The first of these three categories is the professional one, although professional recognition by the Council of Engineering Institutions as a Chartered Engineer requires supplementation of the academic qualification of a degree by approved practical training and responsible experience. Those in the second category are designated Technician Engineers and in the third Engineering Technicians, and in both cases the vast majority of men concerned are in employment and pursue their college studies on a 'sandwich' basis involving day release on one or more days per week, often plus evening study, or block release for periods of up to six months per year.

---

\* Professor A. R. Ubbelohde presented the late Lord Jackson's paper at the Symposium.

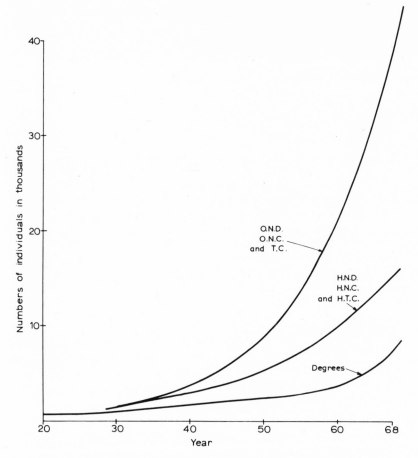

Fig. 1. Annual output of qualified Engineers and Technologists, and of their technical supporting staffs.

In 1968 the outputs at the Technician Engineer and Engineering Technician levels were about twice and five times respectively that of prospective Chartered Engineers. These ratios are not strictly additive in respect of additions to the stock of technical supporting manpower since, in the main, those who attain the higher technician qualifications do so following satisfactory completion of the lower level courses a few years previously.

In the same year, 1968, the output of graduate scientists of all kinds was 11,800, a rather larger number than that of graduate engineers and technologists, 8,300. In the science field the courses and national qualifications for qualified supporting staff are not so clearly defined, and I am unable to provide a correspondingly precise figure. I estimate, however, that the annual output is around three times the graduate one.

In toto, therefore, the additions to the stock of graduate engineers, technologists and scientists from the educational system in 1968 was 20,100, and of their nationally qualified technical supporting staffs around 75,000. The latter figure should be supplemented, though to an unquantifiable extent, by other men and women who complete technican courses organised by their employers, notable examples being the Armed Forces, the British Broadcasting Corporation, and the Coal Board.

## GROWTH OF THE ACTIVE STOCK OF GRADUATE AND GRADUATE EQUI-VALENT ENGINEERS, TECHNOLOGISTS AND SCIENTISTS DURING THE POST-WAR PERIOD

This growth is shown in Fig. 2, and reveals an increase in active stock over the period 1946-68 from about 120,000 to 355,000. This increase, which takes into account losses from the stock by death, retirement, emigration and withdrawal for other reasons, is due not only to the rising graduate output, but also to the fact that a substantial proportion of those possessing Higher National Diploma and Certificate qualifications have pursued more advanced studies to the point of satisfying the examination requirements of the professional institutions, and thereby acquiring graduate equivalent status. The recent decision of the Council of Engineering Institutions to insist on attainment of a degree for this purpose, however, will largely remove this transitional flow in the future, though it will be compensated by increasing participation in degree courses on either a full-time or sandwich basis.

Unfortunately, the available data for technical supporting staff over the years is much more limited. It will no doubt suffice, however, to give the figures provided by the 1968 survey carried out for a large sector of employment by the Committee on Manpower Resources for Science and Technology. This showed that within the sector surveyed the number of employees possessing graduate or graduate equivalent qualifications was about 240,000, and the number performing technician functions, as described in the questionnaire, was around 700,000. On the other hand, only about 40% of the latter possessed a nationally recognised technician qualification such as I have described—the remaining 60% are no doubt promoted craftsmen and operatives, well qualified because of their skill, experience and personal qualities to perform duties falling within the technician function if at the lower level of technical sophistication. While it must, I think, be recognised that the contribution of technical supporting manpower is by no means so clearly relateable to academic qualification as in the case of the professional engineer, technologist and scientists, nevertheless the increasing complexity of the problems of modern industry is demanding of this supporting staff a much enhanced understanding of the technical and organisational issued involved, and is placing a premium on participation in appropriate courses of systematic study and the attainment of the associated qualifications.

## THE AGE DISTRIBUTION OF THE ACTIVE STOCK OF GRADUATE AND GRADUATE EQUIVALENT ENGINEERS, AND THE CHANGING NATURE OF THEIR RESPONSIBILITIES WITH AGE

Figure 3 shows the distribution by age group among a 10% sample of the Chartered Engineer members of the constituent institutions of the Council of Engineering Institutions, and subdivides them into three categories—those employed on essentially technical work; those engaged in lower and middle management; and those who have entered upper management. The sample could not include, a corresponding proportion of those, mainly young people, who though qualified academically and also in respect of training and responsible experience, have not yet chosen to join one or other of the constituent institutions. An estimate of these, shown by the broken curve, has been added to the total number, and it seems reasonable to suppose that this addition

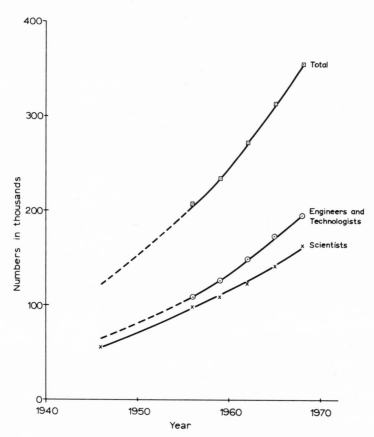

Fig. 2. Active stocks of graduate and graduate equivalent
Engineers, Technologists and Scientists.

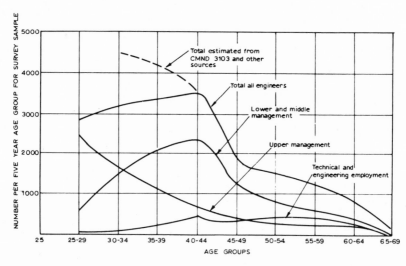

Fig. 3. Age distribution of Chartered Engineers 1966

would have its main effect on the technical employment curve, and enhance the concentration of activity of the younger age groups on work of this kind. There are also not included those, still younger in age, who though qualified academically have not yet satisfied the training and/or experience requirements for Chartered Engineer recognition.

It will be seen that the number engaged dominantly in technical work—in research, development and design—decreases rapidly with age and the number involved in managerial responsibilities increases correspondingly. Having said this, one can not find the distinction between these sub-divisions particularly meaningful, since increasing maturity in technical matters inevitably carries with it increasing responsibility for the work of other people and therefore involvement in managerial matters. The difference in very many cases then is one of degree rather than of a clear cut change in the nature of individual activity. But however the point be interpreted, the question which this diagram seems to raise is—what is going to happen to the large concentration of men within the under 40 years of age group as it moves forward with advancing years? It is not possible to forecast quantitatively how it will come to distribute itself between continued dominant devotion to technical work and movement into middle and upper management. But it is easy enough to forecast some of the considerations which will affect this distribution and the effectiveness with which the relevant duties and responsibilities will be performed.

## WHAT NEEDS TO BE DONE

Though different words are likely to have been used, the point will already have been clearly made in earlier papers, that the attainment of a degree in engineering, technology or science in the early twenties can no longer be regarded as the end of the process of formal education; and that this early preparation must be supplemented at intervals during a career by participation in further courses, as a means of assisting the adaptation to changing scientific and technological situations, of ensuring the maintenance of professional competence and also as an integral part of career development. Failing this, many persons age 30 and older are going to find themselves increasingly embarrassed by lack of adequate understanding of the new analytical and other techniques with which their younger colleagues are familiar. This will operate to the detriment of their own contribution, but it may also seriously retard, or inhibit, the creation of an environment in which these younger members can give satisfying expression to their knowledge and enthusiasm—relatively immature, in other respects, though they may be.

Much of what needs to be learnt is available in the increasing profusion of books and journals, and can be acquired by individual initiative. Indeed without considerable and sustained initiative little of lasting value is likely to be achieved. But even where this exists, a well presented synthesis of a new or developing subject by carefully chosen experts can be of great assistance; and where it does not exist sufficiently of self volition, the professional institutions should stimulate it by requiring evidence of participation in courses of further study, or of other evidence of the maintenance of professional competence, in respect of acceptability for transfer to the higher grades of membership.

There are aspects of management which need to be learnt systematically as well as others that can be gained only by experience, and there are some of course—though not as many as they themselves think—who possess all the necessary qualities by natural endowment. A certificate in management studies does not by itself make a manager, but most of those who possess managerial potentialities would become the better managers by acquiring one.

But I want to take an even wider view than this. I want many more of our graduate engineers, technologists and scientists to see themselves as concerned with the optimum deployment of resources—of men and their ideas as well as of materials—to the achievement of desirable objectives; as concerned with the application of scientific principles through appropriate techniques with due regard to economic, sociological and political considerations. I want, in fact, a rapidly increasing number of those shown in Figure 3 as below 40 years of age—and the corresponding scientists for whom unfortunately I do not have corresponding data—to become involved in the upper management not only of our industries but of our communal affairs.

The Duke of Edinburgh expressed the point in a recent address as follows:

"At this moment in our history when the whole of our existence is dominated by the progress of engineering, technology and science it is absolutely essential that people educated in these fields should have a wider responsibility for the conduct of our affairs."

The success of our growing provision for in-career education should be judged as much, if not more, by its contribution to this objective as by its production of better engineers, technologists and scientists in the purely professional sense, important though the latter may be. Already our achievements in science and technology have run ahead of the ability of the community to adapt itself to the sociological consequences of their impact. This does not mean that the progress of science and technology should be slowed down, but that its direction and objectives should, in part at least, be changed. The time has surely arrived when a starting point should be not a new scientific or technological idea but the selection of a major social problem, either already upon us or likely soon to arise, and the detailed formulation of the contributions which engineering, technology and science might make—will indeed need to make—to its resolution. An outstanding example is the problem of urban planning. Increasingly large urban concentrations will come to characterize not only the present largely industrialized countries but the developing ones as well. It is difficult to think of a contemporary scientific or engineering discipline which does not have a part to play in the unravelling of this problem. It will require of the engineers, technologists and scientists concerned close cooperation with representatives of many other disciplines, and demand of all of them studies extending well beyond the range of their undergraduate curricula.

This example is cited only by way of illustration of the fact that in discussing in-career education we are concerned not only with the preparation of individuals for, and with their adaptation to, changing scientific and technological situations per se but also with their involvement in, and responsibilities towards, the changing sociological situation which follows sequentially. In this connection it must not be supposed that the need is limited to the graduate component of qualified manpower. Though in detailed content and in intellectual standard the need is no doubt different at the level of supporting manpower, it is of no less importance at this level. This means that in the engineering, technological and scientific field alone the United Kingdom has on its plate the in-career educational problems of a present active stock of well over one million people.

## WHOSE RESPONSIBILITY?

In approaching a consideration of this question it is important to remember that we are dealing with individuals. Within the limited part of the United Kingdom situation I have concentrated on, there are some 350,000 graduate scientists, technologists and engineers and at least 1 million technical supporting staff, covering the age spectrum from say 25 to 65 years of age, and a great diversity of levels of intellectual ability, of mental and manual skills, and of personal qualities. The problem at issue is how to enhance the in-career contribution and assist the in-career development of individuals, while recognising that, though individuals, they are members of teams engaged in corporate activities aimed at clearly defined objectives. It is, I suggest, a pre-requisite for the progress of a corporate activity that the participating individuals must have a sense of personal responsibility towards it, and therefore a sense of responsibility to maintain and enhance their own competence but also that of their associates, especially their more junior colleagues. Each of us can remember men who at various stages of our careers have stimulated, if not inspired, us by their encouragement and example. And yet it is disappointing to observe how many men are apparently unable or unwilling to appreciate that the difficulties and frustrations their junior colleagues are experiencing are much the same as they themselves had complained about at an earlier date, and to recognise that they have a responsibility toward their junior colleagues and subordinates. Sir Arthur Fleming, whom I succeeded many years later as Director of Research and Education in the Metropolitan Vickers Electrical Company in Manchester, once said to me "a poor environment can rapidly convert a first class man into a mediocre one—if he stays." And it need hardly be stated that the nature of an environment is largely determined by the senior men in it.

Little of lasting value will be achieved in the absence of considerable and sustained individual initiative. The degree of individual initiative is usually very closely related to the encouragement and stimulation of more senior colleagues. This applies not only to the doing better of existing jobs but also to the preparation for doing new ones as the need or possibility arises. Taken through to its conclusion the responsibility applies particularly to the top managements of all organisations. In my experience the vast majority of senior executives seem far too well satisfied that what they are doing in this respect is adequate, and too self-persuaded that what needs to be done, can only be done effectively within the confines of their own organisation. More often than not, I have been sceptical of their concept of adequacy and of the ability of their organisation by itself to satisfy the requirements of a more realistic assessment. In my experience few organisations are providing—or indeed are capable of providing—comprehensive re-education and re-training schemes within themselves.

This raises the question as to whether organisations which are attempting to re-train, and which are therefore likely to lose some of their well trained staff members to organisations which are not, should carry the whole of the consequential expense. The practice of transfer fees for professional footballers is hardly applicable to industrial employment, but at any rate some compensation is provided in the United Kingdom under the levy-grant schemes operated by the Industrial Training Boards established under the 1964 Industrial Training Act. The Engineering Industries Training Board, for example, imposes a levy of 2½% of the wages and salary budgets of all the firms falling within its scope, amounting in total to around £80 million per annum. It then refunds this income, less the costs of administration, to those firms which are carrying out approved schemes of training either of apprentice recruits or of mature employees.

It is difficult, however, to persuade the Industrial Training Boards to make grants in aid of the participation of mature employees in full-time advanced courses organised within the universities, colleges of technology or technical colleges, even when, as is increasingly the case, these are provided on the initiative of, and conducted in close collaboration with, industry, and when much of the teaching work is carried out by carefully selected senior staff members drawn from industry. In consequence the whole of the costs—continued payment of salary, living expenses if away from home and course fees—for participants in post-experience courses conducted in educational institutions fall upon the employer. The course fees can be high since, as distinct from the normal sessional courses which are dominantly financed from governmental or local authority sources, educational institutions are seeking to make their post-experience courses self-supporting. The net result is that the growth of these university and college courses, though substantial, is affecting a much smaller proportion of the stock of the qualified manpower in science, technology and engineering, and for a much shorter time, than the rapidly changing situation seems to me to demand.

The courses just mentioned vary in duration from a few days to several months full time. In addition the colleges of technology and technical colleges, but not the universities, provide a wide range of advanced part-time day and evening courses. Their sponsorship and regional coordination is the responsibility of a number of Regional Advisory Councils, and their financing, over and above fees, that of the relevant Local Authority. These courses attract in aggregate a much larger number of students than the corresponding full-time college courses, and the evening students concerned participate largely of their own volition and pay the associated fees out of their own pockets.

The results of a sample survey of graduate engineers and technologists carried out two years ago by the Ministry of Technology are to be found in the Appendix. Unfortunately, the data does not distinguish between courses organised within the employing organisation and those provided by outside educational institutions. It will be evident, however, that the bulk of the courses are of quite short duration, and in my opinion only the fringe of the problem has yet been touched. I have been unable to obtain comparable information for technical supporting manpower, but have no hesitation in saying that outside the domain of employment, the provision of in-career courses is as yet minimal.

The participation of selected senior representatives of industry in the planning and, as lecturers, in the conduct of post-experience courses is an extremely important feature of the courses. I do not wish to under-rate the contribution which can be, and is, made to the teaching work by the full-time staff members of the universities and colleges concerned in saying that many of them lack sufficient responsible experience of industrial life, and are in insufficiently close touch with present-day industrial problems, to carry more than a part of the responsibility for them. Fortunately, this is widely recognised and the appointment of representatives of industry, government establishments and the public utilities as Special Lecturers and Professors has become a general practice. It will be readily appreciated, however, that the men most wanted are often the ones most deeply involved in the affairs of their respective organisations and are therefore difficult, if not impossible, to recruit.

Credit should be given for the contributions made by the professional institutions, typified by the Institution of Electrical Engineers with a membership of about 60,000, in this field. During the period February to May 1970 the London centre of this Institution organised 120 evening lectures and associated discussions with an average attendance of between 2-300, and during June, July and September there are to be 10 Conferences of 3 days average duration. In addition it has introduced a number of correspondence courses dealing with new developments in the subject of electrical engineering, and it proposes to extend this facility considerably if the initial courses are well supported. This is a step towards what I regard as an inevitable and urgent decision to require evidence of successful participation in post-graduate courses, or other evidence of the maintenance of professional competence, as a condition of election or transfer to the higher grades of membership.

## CONCLUSION

In the preceding attempt to answer the question 'Whose Responsibility?' I have pointed to the individual, to his employer, to the educational bodies and to the professional institutions. I have not pointed specifically to central government. Central government is, of course, involved in so far as it provides university finance via the Department of Education and Science for allocation through the University Grants Committee; college of technology and technical college finance via the same department for allocation by local authorities; and supervision of the Industrial Training Boards by the Department of Employment and Productivity. But there is no centre of responsibility for assessing the magnitude and detailed nature of the overall problem and for planning, coordinating and ensuring the adequate financing of the means of its resolution. Frankly, I do not have a clear idea what form it might take, and shall look forward to hearing what might have been conceived or achieved elsewhere.

In conclusion it should be noted that no reference has been made to full-time sessional post-graduate university courses and research activities leading to Masters and Doctors degrees. There is no intent to overlook their importance as affording an extended preparation for entry into certain kinds of career, notably in research and development and in teaching work. But for the great majority of persons there still lie ahead some 35–40 years of employment, and though these participants may be better prepared than most others to find their own way through the problems of adjustment and adaptation to changing situations, the differences are of degree rather than kind.

**APPENDIX**

Summary of the results of a sample survey of graduate and graduate equivalent engineers and technologists carried out by the Ministry of Technology in 1968.

### Nature of the post-experience courses

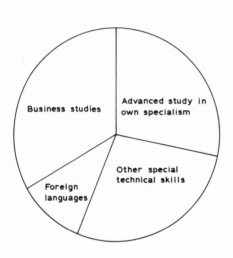

Nearly one-third of the courses taken were business studies, including management. These were taken by higher proportions in the older age groups than in the younger ones, but there was still considerable participation even by the youngest engineers: 25 per cent of all courses taken by those under 30 were business studies, compared with 39 per cent of courses taken by those aged 50 and over.

The number of courses concerned with advanced studies in own specialism and with other technical skills were nearly equal, each accounting for 28 per cent of all courses. On the whole, the younger engineers were more involved in these than the older ones.

Compared with these, the number of courses in foreign languages was small, accounting for 11 per cent of all courses taken. They were taken predominantly by older engineers.

| | All courses | | Advanced study in own specialism | Other special technical skills | Foreign Languages | Business Studies |
|---|---|---|---|---|---|---|
| All courses | 10269 | | 2898 | 2882 | 1095 | 3394 |
| | | % | % | % | % | % |
| Courses taken by engineers stating age | 10254 | 100 | 28.2 | 28.1 | 10.7 | 33.1 |
| Under 25 | 756 | 100 | 39.2 | 28.4 | 6.6 | 25.8 |
| 25–29 | 2094 | 100 | 36.0 | 32.5 | 7.4 | 24.2 |
| 30–34 | 2032 | 100 | 29.3 | 27.7 | 9.5 | 33.0 |
| 35–39 | 1634 | 100 | 25.4 | 30.3 | 9.1 | 35.3 |
| 40–44 | 1624 | 100 | 21.6 | 26.0 | 14.4 | 38.0 |
| 45–49 | 1206 | 100 | 22.6 | 25.7 | 12.6 | 39.1 |
| 50–54 | 507 | 100 | 24.8 | 21.3 | 15.2 | 38.7 |
| 55–59 | 281 | 100 | 17.8 | 22.1 | 18.9 | 41.3 |
| 60 and over | 120 | 100 | 20.0 | 19.2 | 27.5 | 33.3 |

## Graduate and graduate equivalent engineers taking
## post-experience courses

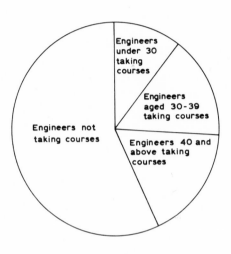

The courses recorded on the questionnaire were taken within the twelve months preceding the survey and were limited to post-experience training. In considering the results, it is necessary to distinguish between numbers of engineers taking courses and the number of courses they took. Many engineers took more than one course, so the number of courses (10,269) is greater than the number of engineers taking them (70610).

During this period of twelve months, 38 per cent of all engineers took at least one training course. As would be expected, higher proportions of the younger than the older engineers took courses: more than half of those under 30 took courses, and the proportion then drops with age to 9 per cent of those aged over 60.

|  | All engineers | Engineers taking courses | Engineers taking courses in each age group per cent |
|---|---|---|---|
| All engineers | 18497 | 7061 | 38.2 |
| Engineers stating age | 18444 | 7051 | 38.2 |
|  |  |  |  |
| Under 25 | 732 | 458 | 62.6 |
| 25–29 | 2762 | 1407 | 50.9 |
| 30–34 | 3202 | 1409 | 44.0 |
| 35–39 | 2789 | 1135 | 40.7 |
| 40–44 | 3197 | 1166 | 36.5 |
| 45–49 | 2375 | 845 | 35.6 |
| 50–54 | 1306 | 344 | 26.3 |
| 55–59 | 1134 | 200 | 17.6 |
| 60 and over | 947 | 87 | 9.2 |

### Length of the post-experience courses

Courses in foreign languages were nearly all part-time courses, and they tended to stretch over long periods. Courses in other technical skills split almost equally between full-time and part-time and were mainly comparatively short. The other two classes, advanced studies in own specialisms and business studies, involved more full-time than part-time courses, and were mainly comparatively short. In spite of this, however, 24 per cent of the advanced studies and 21 per cent of the business studies courses lasted between nineteen weeks and a full year.

FULL TIME COURSES

  One week courses

  Two to six week courses

  Seven to eighteen week courses

  Courses of more than eighteen weeks

PART TIME COURSES

  One week courses

  Two to six week courses

  Seven to eighteen week courses

  Courses of more than eighteen weeks

| | All courses | | Advanced study in own specialism | Other special technical skills | Foreign Languages | Business Studies |
|---|---|---|---|---|---|---|
| | | % | % | % | % | % |
| All courses | 10269 | 100 | 28.2 | 28.1 | 10.7 | 33.0 |
| Full time | 5163 | 100 | 32.3 | 28.5 | 0.9 | 38.3 |
| 1 week | 3117 | 100 | 31.2 | 29.4 | .0.1 | 39.3 |
| 2–6 weeks | 1421 | 100 | 26.4 | 30.7 | 1.2 | 41.7 |
| 7–18 weeks | 277 | 100 | 38.3 | 21.7 | 3.6 | 36.4 |
| Over 18 weeks | 348 | 100 | 61.5 | 17.0 | 5.2 | 16.4 |
| Part time | 5106 | 100 | 24.1 | 27.6 | 20.5 | 27.8 |
| 1 week . | 1147 | 100 | 20.7 | 35.8 | 1.2 | 42.2 |
| 2–6 weeks | 629 | 100 | 29.4 | 42.3 | 8.4 | 19.9 |
| 7–18 weeks | 1195 | 100 | 26.7 | 38.9 | 21.3 | 13.1 |
| Over 18 weeks | 2135 | 100 | 22.9 | 12.6 | 34.0 | 30.5 |

# Professional Updating for the Advancement of National Purpose:
# An Analysis of U.S.Government Activities

Carl M. York    Executive Office of the President,
                Washington, D.C.

The significant fact about the role of professional updating for the advancement of national purposes is that it is relatively of little concern in the United States today. On the face of it, this may seem to defy good sense and possibly to risk a dangerous lag in knowledge and capabilities. But viewed in the context of America's unusual situation in higher education today, particularly regarding scientific and technical training, it becomes clear that it is a very natural attitude. Let us, therefore, consider professional updating within this broader framework, first tracing the history of federal involvement with higher education and then examining the problems and opportunities currently facing the United States.

## FEDERAL INVOLVEMENT IN HIGHER EDUCATION

Federal involvement with higher education has been characterized by a high degree of ambivalence. While higher education has badly needed the monetary support of the federal government, the universities have been reluctant to accept it for fear of losing their independence. In spite of this ambivalence, however, a unique system has grown up. Although George Washington proposed that a federal university be built in the District of Columbia in the late eighteenth century, his suggestion was soundly defeated. Other subsequent attempts failed until, in 1862, the Morrill Act was passed. This established the land grant college system, providing for colleges in each state to teach the 'agricultural and mechanic arts.' Later legislation supplemented the support for these schools by establishing agricultural experiment stations and a network of country agents to disseminate and apply the latest research results at local levels. A still later addition to these laws provided for the training of reserve officers for the armed services. As each successive step was taken, the issue of federal control was hotly debated and carefully resolved by appropriate safeguards and compromises.

Although the foundation of this structure was slowly and laboriously laid over eighty years, it was radically changed by World War II. By Executive Order, President Roosevelt established the Manhattan Project, and laboratories sprang up on several university campuses. The work of this project, which led to the development of atomic weapons and nuclear power, is well known. A similar laboratory, called the Radiation Laboratory, was established at about the same time to develop the British invention of radar. These two scientific and technological enterprises drew heavily upon university faculties and students, and in so doing established an intimate working relationship between the Executive Branch of the Federal Government and the universities. The mutual advantages of this new partnership triggered the post-war expansion of federally funded campus research.

But once more the ambivalence of the American mind was apparent. Most faculty members were reluctant as a matter of principle to do research for the military. These are patriotic men who in peacetime feel that it is inappropriate for their work to be related to the military establishment. Immediately after the war, therefore, they began pressing for a civilian agency to support scientific research and in 1950 the National Science Foundation was created. Although it was important to have a civilian agency as the primary support for basic research, it was even more significant that the development of the relationship between the universities and the federal government was once more in the arena of open Congressional debate rather than a matter of Executive Order as in the case of the Manhattan Project.

A new turning point in the history of federal support for higher education came in 1957 when the Russians launched the first Sputnik. The growing national concern over this achievement by a rival power was expressed somewhat later in 1960 by President Kennedy when he pledged to 'land a man upon the surface of the moon within this decade.' The federal government responded by conducting a manpower study to identify the means by which this new goal could be achieved. This study was carried out under the auspices of the President's Science Advisory Committee (PSAC) and is known as the Gilliland Report (1). It not only projected the technically trained manpower pool that would be needed, but made it clear that if the federal government were to use a substantial fraction of that pool, it had an obligation to support the training of a fair share of that manpower. The result was an extremely successful expanded training program spread over several federal agencies—NSF, HEW, and NASA. A new PSAC study (2) indicates that the number of trained scientists and engineers projected by the Gilliland Report was actually achieved by 1968.

Thus in early 1970 the United States was suddenly confronted with an excess of technically and scientifically trained manpower. In retrospect, the reasons are clear. The needed number of PhD's was already produced two years ago. But the university system is in high gear, currently producing new PhD's at a rate six times greater than the growth rate of the Nation's population. Thus we find the predicted job market saturated and the rate of production of new graduates continuing at full speed. The problem of unemployment has been compounded, moreover, by a suddenly diminishing job market. Decreased federal spending on the space program—men have been landed on the moon—and decreased federal spending on large defense systems has substantially reduced the number of jobs in the aerospace industry.

Another shrinking job market is in higher education. The fact is that it is not possible to justify the continued expansion of the number of higher learning institutions in the United States. The argument can best be understood in terms of Figure 1. The topmost curve, labelled 'College-Age Population,' shows the time variation of the number of young people between the ages of 18 and 21 in the US population. Although the curve only projects to 1985, the number of children born last year makes it possible to extend the curve to 1987; the number of births is known, and this can be corrected for actuarial mortality rates, immigration and emigration. The most striking feature of this curve is the downward trend after 1980, reflecting a sharp decline in the number of births over the past nine years.

The lower curve shows total enrollment in higher education. The solid part of the curve was taken from the Office of Education statistical tables (3), and the broken line labelled I represents the OE projection for 1970 onward. This year (1970) is quite important because it shows the achievement of 50% enrollment of the entire

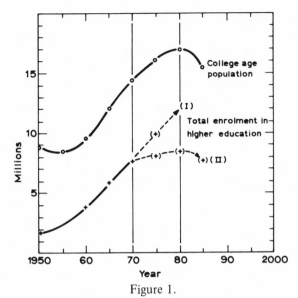

Figure 1.

Projection of College Age Population and Total Enrollment in Higher Education

college-age population in institutions of higher education. The question is: can we continue to enroll a larger fraction of this age group in our institutions of higher education without changing those institutions? Or should we accept the possibility that only half of this age group *should be* enrolled in what is basically a four year liberal arts program? Such a limitation is indicated by the branch of the lower curve labelled II, and could be justified on the ground that, by definition, half of any age group has an IQ of less than 100. Furthermore, the verbal skills required to survive in a liberal arts program are very similar to the verbal skills used to measure IQ. What then is implied by enrolling more than half the college-age group in institutions of higher learning? Should we try to give them a liberal arts education or, as has been suggested in the Higher Education Act of 1970, should we provide for more technical and para-professional training opportunities at the post-secondary level? If we accept a 50% limit on enrollees in higher education, curve II indicates that we now have all of the liberal arts and graduate schools needed. Hence the job market for PhD's in higher education is greatly reduced.

In summary, the United States is confronted with a substantial oversupply and overproduction of well-trained technicians, scientists and engineers. At the same time, the job market is contracting. In this situation professional updating is not so important to federal policy makers as professional retraining and transitional training.

## A REASSESSMENT OF THE FEDERAL ROLE IN HIGHER EDUCATION

The foregoing situation has forced the federal government carefully to reassess its role in higher education. Historically, there are two basic reasons why the federal government has become involved in higher education in general, and in science and technology in particular. The United States Constitution requires the federal government to provide for the general welfare of the people as well as for their defense. We have already seen that the government purchased research from universities essentially for the purpose first, to improve agriculture and then to provide for the country's defense during and at the end of World War II. This rationale is a basic part of the support of research and training in the universities today. In providing for the general welfare the federal government through the various land-grant college and education acts has justified its role in the direct subsidy of education at all levels. The changes currently taking place in the federal posture are dictated largely by the overproduction of highly trained manpower in almost all fields, from nuclear physics to English literature. Because this has come at a time of budgetary stringency, the first question that has arisen is: should the federal government continue subsidizing graduate students through fellowships, traineeships and reasearch assistantships?

Although there is enormous pressure at present to hold down federal spending, a system will most probably emerge which provides a balance between the various forms of support. The first will be competitive national fellowships which will set standards of excellence and provide national recognition for our brightest young people. There will be traineeships in specific professions deemed to have manpower shortages, including computer scientists and medical doctors. Some research assistantships funded directly from research project grants will also continue to be available. A newly expanded loan program will serve as simply another channel of student support and may dominate as a support mechanism within the next few years.

The goal of a post-secondary education for all will continue to be the watchword. However, as Figure 1 shows, a saturation in terms of the number of students to receive such training will begin by about 1980. This universal post-secondary education experience will begin to emphasize vocational training and does not imply a substantial expansion of the liberal arts education which characterizes higher education in the United States today.

## THE FEDERAL ROLE IN PROFESSIONAL UPDATING

The present 'oversupply' of PhD's is clearly a problem of great concern. It can be looked upon as a great opportunity to move very bright, talented and highly trained professionals from the classical fields of scholarship into areas of new concern such as the environment, urban transportation and development of the inner city. Clearly, retraining and transitional programs for professionals will be the key to using the present burgeoning manpower pool; professional updating per se will be of secondary importance.

What federal programs are available to help carry out this transition from one field to another? There are the well known programs of the Atomic Energy Commission to train those holding the bachelor's degree in science to become nuclear engineers, radiation technicians and health physicists. The National Institutes of Health has a broad spectrum of trainee programs which do everything from schooling experts in research animal handling to providing physicians an opportunity to obtain PhD-level research experience in a multitude of fields. The newer agencies such as the Department of Housing and Urban Development have established multi-disciplinary programs designed to attack the multi-faceted problems of our cities. 'Conglomerate' degree programs involving some work in the varied fields of sociology, economics, systems analysis, public health and a few others have been introduced in the universities to respond to these national needs. The Department of Transportation has set up similar programs in urban transportation to provide student support for relevant programs of study. More recently the new Environmental Quality Council has indicated that it will encourage collegiate study of this vital subject.

However, one should not be misled by such a list of new opportunities. All of these embryonic programs provide for a comparatively small number of students when compared to the large numbers of graduate students now in United States universities and the large number of unemployed professionals from the aerospace and defense industries. Although these programs in selected areas of national interest have been started, an entire federal budget for the fiscal year 1971 was submitted to the Congress with the explicit provision that no new traineeships in the basic fields of science be provided. This provision was included as a money-saving device. Although some of these traineeships were restored by Presidential action, the current philosophy for the fiscal year 1972 is to support only those traineeships which are relevant to programs of national need. Many feel that it is not possible to predict what areas of national concern will be important five to seven years from now. Yet the time required to produce a PhD is of this duration. Perhaps budgetary pressures will be recognized as a very inefficient way to establish policies needed to train students. At the moment, however, this rationale prevails. The result is that there are a relatively small number of poorly funded, not very well thought out programs for training college graduates and retraining professionals in the new areas of national concern.

## CONCLUSION

From the foregoing description of United States government activities, one must conclude that until the new programs can begin to function, all of these man power programs are in a state of limbo. As momentum builds up in the pursuit of these new goals, one can hope that a revitalization of the country as a whole will occur. At present professional updating in the usual sense is not so much a concern as transitional training.

## REFERENCES

(1) The President's Science Advisory Committee. *Meeting manpower needs in science and technology* (The White House, Government Printing Office, Washington, DC, 1962)
(2) Terman, F. E. *The supply of scientific and engineering manpower—surplus or shortage?* (Unpublished paper prepared for a subpanel on academic science of the President's Science Advisory Committee, May, 1970)
(3) Simon, K. A., Fulham, M. G. *Projections of educational statistics to 1977-78 (Office of Education/Dept. of Health, Education and Welfare, US Government Printing Office, OE-10030-68)*

# La Formation en Cours de Carrière dans le Cadre des Travaux de l'OCDE (Current OECD Studies on In-Career Education of Highly Qualified Manpower)

**L. Ter-Davtian   OCDE, Paris**

Le phénomène de l'accélération de l'histoire, mis en évidence par Daniel Halévy, s'est considérablement amplifié depuis quelque temps par suite des progrès rapides des sciences et des techniques. Ce n'est plus entre deux générations successives qu'apparaissent des différences notables dans les modes de vie et d'activité, mais entre les diverses étapes de la vie même d'un seul individu. L'un des aspects les plus frappants de cette mutation est la transformation des métiers et des professions. Sous des appellations parfois nouvelles, mais le plus souvent identiques, les hommes exercent des activités dont le contenu évolue à une cadence telle qu'un homme, au cours de sa vie active, est amené à changer plusieurs fois de métier. L'apparition de nouveaux métiers comme celui de programmeur sur ordinateur ou de spécialiste de l'analyse des systèmes, attire davantage l'attention que la mutation profonde que subit le contenu de la plupart de nos activités professionnelles: on sait, par exemple, que l'industrie chimique réalisera dans 10 ans près de la moitié de son chiffre d'affaires par la vente de produits que nous ne connaissons pas encore; il est donc certain que le travail de l'ingénieur chimiste sera alors différent de ce qu'il est aujourd'hui. Même une activité comme la médecine dont l'appellation et l''image' sociale semblent rester immuables n'est plus aujourd'hui ce qu'elle était il y a 10 ou 20 ans et sera encore différente bien avant la fin du siècle. La découverte des antibiotiques et d'une multitude de médicaments nouveaux, les progrès de la chirurgie, le perfection nement des appareils d'investigation permis par l'électronique, sans parler de l'utilisation des mémoires des ordinateurs donnent à l'activité médicale des traits sensiblement différents de ce qu'elle était naguère en dépit de l'apparente stabilité que l'organisation séculaire de la profession tendrait à faire croire.

L' exemple de la médecine est intéressant car il illustre l'antinomie croissante entre le caractère changeant d'une profession et le besoin de stabilité dans leur situation sociale qu'éprouvent ceux qui l'exercent. Le réflexe du type 'défense des droits,' bien conforme à la nature humaine, s'observe dans toutes les classes de la socièté, et se trouve à l'origine de la résistance au changement d'où naissent les conflits. La pression des réalités finit parfois par imposer le changement mais au prix de souffrances engendrant parfois une agitation sociale qui ne peut laisser indifférents les pouvoirs publics. La reconnaissance d'une compétence professionnelle assise sur un diplôme initial, attestant une qualification au moment où l'individu entre dans la vie active, ne peut en effet être mainte nue tout au long de la carrière que grâce à un effort permanent d'adaptation aux exigences constamment changeantes des fonctions et cet effort est souvent d'une ampleur telle qu'il dépasse la capacité du seul individu.

Depuis une dizaine d'années l'O.C.D.E. s'est engagée dans l'étude des problèmes que pose la transformation des métiers et de ses conséquences sur l'appareil éducatif entendu au sens large. Il existe maintenant dans beaucoup de pays Membres, des groupes nationaux dont le statut et les caractéristiques sont variables mais qui ont pour point commun de permettre une concertation entre les pouvoirs publics, les autorités responsables de l'enseignement sous ses diverses formes et aux divers niveaux, et les responsables des activités économiques. Ces groupes ont entrepris, notamment, des études visant à mettre à la disposition des instances investies du pouvoir de décision les informations objectives dont elles ont besoin pour élaborer, en toute connaissance de cause. les politiques de leur pays en matière d'utilisation des ressources humaines.

L'objet de la présente communication est de donner un aperçu de ces activités.

Comme le thème principal choisi pour le symposium est l'obsolescence du personnel de haute qualification, il paraît utile de faire une analyse de la notion même d'obsolescence avant d'examiner à titre d'exemple, quelques-unes des études destinées à alimenter la documentation d'une Conférence Intergouvernmentale sur l'Utilisation du Personnel Hautement Qualifié (PHQ) que l'O.C.D.E. organise dans le courant de l'année prochaine.

## LA NOTION D'OBSOLESCENCE

Dans sa première acception, l'obsolescence désigne le fait que les connaissances d'un individu, dans un domaine donné, soient dépassées par l'état actuel de la science et de la technique, par suite des progrès intervenus dans sa spécialité depuis le moment où il les a acquises au cours de ses études. Combattre l'obsolescence, entendu dans ce sens étroit, consisterait donc à donner à l'individu la possibilité d'étudier une matière donnée dans l'état actuel de son évolution.

En d'autres termes, le problème posé est celui de l'acquisition d'un savoir supplémentaire qui s'ajoute ou se substitue aux connaissances acquises antérieurement et rafraîchit celles de ces connaissances, encore valables, qui auraient été oubliées.

Quel est le nombre d'individus qui, pour l'exercice de leur profession, ont besoin de connaître l'état actuel d'une matière telle qu'elle est enseignée actuellement? Peu de recherches ont été effectuées pour parvenir à une telle évaluation et les données que nous possédons sont en général relatives à des secteurs limités. Les informations que nous possédons nous permettent de supposer que le pourcentage d'individus touchés par ce type particulier d'obsolescence est relativement faible.

Cette circonstance s'explique par le fait que la population de personnel hautement qualifié comprend d'une part ceux qui se sont spécialisés dans une matière donnée et qui s'ils sont engagés dàns une activité de recherche—ont même participé au progrès ou en ont eu immédiatement connaissance à l'occasion de leur activité professionnelle. D'autre part, il y a tous ceux qui se trouvent en un point de leur carrière où les fonctions qu'ils replissent ne comportent plus la mise en oeuvre directe de certaines connaissances à la manière des jeunes diplômés: il n'y a, en réalité, pas concurrence entre ces jeunes diplômés et les diplômés d'il y a 10 ou 15 ans ayant suivi une carrière normale. Ce n'est pas à dire que ces derniers doivent ignorer les progrès accomplis dans leur spécialité, mais le genre de connaissance qu'ils doivent en avoir se situe au niveau de l'information: ils doivent savoir ce qui a été accompli et l'usage qui peut en être fait afin d'en faire mettre en application ce qui peut être utile à leur service. Ajoutons que ce genre d'information leur est nécessaire non seulement dans la spécialité qui fut la leur, mais également dans d'autres.

Il existe, dans un livre déjà ancien publié il y a plus d'un demi-siècle par Fayol (1), une série de graphiques colorés montrant les types de connaissances et d'aptitudes dont a besoin un ingénieur au fur et à mesure que sa carrière évolue et l'appelle à remplir des fonctions de direction de niveaux de plus en plus élevés. On y voit que le pourcentage de connaissances techniques spécialisées diminue graduellement, alors qu'apparaît, pour croître rapidement, le besoin de connaître l'utilisation de techniques variées. Or, dans le meilleur des cas, l'ingénieur n'a eu, au cours de ses études, qu'un aperçu assez général de certaines matières et parfois, lorsqu' il s'agit de problèmes financiers ou administratifs, aucune connaissance tant soit peu approfondie.

Ainsi de la notion d'obsolescence prise dans sa première acception, on passe à une notion beaucoup plus large qui est celle de l'inadaptation d'un individu aux emplois qu'offre la société, inadaptation due bien entendu, dans certains cas, au fait que les connaissances qui lui ont été enseignées sont dépassées par suite de récentes découvertes, mais aussi, dans des cas très nombreux, au fait que la demande de l'économie, pour le type de qualification qu'il possède se trouve réduite, cette réduction provenant de la mutation que subit la société dans son ensemble.

La notion d'obsolescence ainsi entendue dans son sens large d'inadaptation aux besoins de la société comporte des nuances selon les professions et affecte un nombre d'individus variable dans les divers métiers. Chez ceux qui, durant toute leur carrière, restent dans la même branche professionnelle, on est plus proche de la première acception: c'est le cas de certaines professions libérales: l'ingénieur conseil, l'architecte, le médecin, le juriste, pourraient combattre l'obsolescence en étudiant les modifications intervenues dans leur art depuis la fin de leurs études. Dans le cas des individus engagés dans des carrières techniques ou administratives de type salarié, il s'agit surtout d'une inadaptation qui ne saurait être combattue par la seule remise à jour des connaissances déjà apprises ou l'addition de connaissances relevant du même domaine de spécialisation: des compléments parfois considérables sont nécessaires, allant jusqu'à l'apprentissage d'un véritable métier nouveau, comme celui de 'manager.'

Pour mieux connaitre le phénomène, des études et recherches en profondeur seraient nécessaires au moins dans deux directions:
1–Etude des carrières suivies par les individus possédant une qualification et appartenant à différentes professions, afin de déterminer les connaissances et aptitudes effectivement mises en pratique dans l'exercice de leurs fonctions successives et de définir le type de formation nécessaire pour les y adapter.

2–Etude du nombre de personnes touchées ou menacées par tel ou tel type d'obsolescence en vue d'obtenir une évaluation quantitative des besoins. Lorsqu'il s'agira d'inadaptation, il conviendra de pousser l'analyse suffisamment loin pour connaître l'importance des mesures requises pour faire acquérir la compétence correspondante à une fonction donnée. La durée des divers types de formation destinée à faciliter les reconversions serait un élément important pour la détermination des moyens à mettre en oeuvre, mais le problème serait compliqué du fait de la variation de l'adaptabilité de l'individu avec l'âge.

## EXEMPLES D'ETUDES
## SUR LA FORMATION EN COURS DE CARRIERE

A titre d'exemples on présentera ci-dessous trois études particulières qui serviront dans la préparation des documents de base destinés à la conférence sur l'utilisation du PHQ de 1971. Il s'agit d'une part de deux études relatives à des secteurs limités, et d'autre part, d'une étude couvrant l'ensemble de l'industrie d'un pays.

### Etudes concernant des secteurs limités

Ces deux études ont été faites l'une aux Etats-Unis (2) et l'autre en France (3).

Ces études présentent des analogies et des différences qu'il est intéressant de relever:

a) Elles ont été faites toutes les deux à la demande des Gouvernements des pays en question pour permettre aux pouvoirs publics de disposer d'informations objectives.

b) Elles portent sur des secteurs limités de l'activité industrielle et ont utilisé la méthode des questionnaires complétés par des interviews. Celle menée aux Etats-Unis couvre un ensemble d'activités industrielles assez large caractérisées par des transformations profondes dues aux progrès de la science (espace, électronique, chimie, métaux non ferreux). Celle qui a été faite en France se limite à un secteur plus étroit, celui de l'électronique, d'où les auteurs ont cherché à dégager une méthodologie applicable à l'ensemble des secteurs de pointe. L'étude américaine a porté seulement sur 39 entreprises, alors que l'étude française, bien que limitée à un secteur très étroit, a couvert 47 entreprises employant plus de 50% de l'ensemble de l'industrie électronique. Elle peut donc être considérée comme assez représentative de cette industrie particulière alors que l'étude amércaine est une simple étude pilote.

c) Les deux études ont tenté une évaluation des besoins de formation en cours de carrière aussi bien sous l'angle qualitatif que sous l'angle quantitatif. Sur le plan quantitatif les conclusions auxquelles elles sont parvenues sont sensiblement différentes. Cette circonstance s'explique sans doute par la largeur inégale des domaines d'activité et la différence entre les périodes de référence. L'étude américaine aui embrasse des activités assez variées et considère la situation à l'instant de l enquête, conclut que la proportion du PHQ qui a besoin d'une formation complémentaire ne dépasse pas 25%: seul semble être affecté le personnel travaillant dans le secteur de la recherche, du développement et de la conception, qui constitue la moitié de l'ensemble du PHQ employé dans les secteurs industriels considérés. De plus, dans ce groupe même, le personnel réellement affecté est celui qui se trouve avoir terminé ses études depuis plus de 10 ou 15 ans et le nombre de ces individus ne dépasse pas la moitié du personnel total engagé dans la recherche et le développement Ce pourcentage assex faible explique l'opinion des chefs d'entreprises rapportée par les enquêteurs, que l'obsolescence des qualifications constitue rarement un problème de très grande gravité. Il n'a été signalé comme véritablement grave que dans quelques-unes des entreprises soumises à l'enquête et pour un petit nombre de postes, mais dont l'importance, il est vrai, est très grande et justifie les préoccupations des chefs d'entreprises: il s'agit des directeurs techniques, des directeurs de recherche, des spécialistes de l'analyse des systèmes, qui occupent dans les entreprises des positions clés. Les entreprises américaines ont d'ailleurs pris des mesures pour former ce type de personnel par un effort de détection des talents et de formation parfois considérables. En ce qui concerne l'étude française, les chiffres recueillis sont relatifs à des besoins s'étendant sur une période de cinq ans et sont relatifs aux seules industries électroniques. Ils semblent nettement plus élevés.

L'analyse a été faite en tenant compte de 3 éléments: la catégorie profession-nelle, le niveau de la formation de base reçue, le domaine où s'exerce l'activité.

Besoins de recyclage par catégorie professionnelle

| Catégories professionnelles | Pourcentage du personnel touché par l'obsolescence |
|---|---|
| Cadres de direction | 26 % |
| Cadres supérieurs | 68 % |
| Cadres d'exécution | 60 % |
| Techniciens supérieurs | 92 % |
| Techniciens de production | 51 % |

Besoins de recyclage en fonction du niveau de formation de base

| Nivaux de formation | Catégories professionnelles | |
|---|---|---|
| | cadres supérieurs | cadres d'éxécution |
| Grandes écoles ou universités | 53 % | 46 % |
| Ecoles spécialisées | 58 % | 58 % |
| Autodidactes | 49 % | 45 % |

Besoins de recyclage par domaines d'activité

| Domaines d'activité | Effectifs à recycler |
|---|---|
| Recherche fondamentale | 0 % |
| Recherche appliquée | 50 % |
| Etudes des systèmes | 74 % |
| Etudes techniques des produits | 45 % |
| Production | 86 % |
| Gestion administrative | 40 % |
| Vente | |

d) Les deux études ont cherché à comparer les besoins ressentis dans l'industrie aux enseignements offerts par les différentes institutions d'éducation:université, collèges techniques, associations professionnelles, centres de formation publics ou privés. Cependant, alors que l'étude américaine se préoccupe des programmes de formation initiale, l'étude française porte essentiellement sur les programmes dits de recyclage, offerts par ces institutions et dont elle donne une analyse extrêmement détaillée. Sur le plan *qualitatif*, seule l'étude française donne, avec un certain détail, le type de formation complémentaire requis pour combattre certains effets de l'obsolescence, en procédant à une analyse selon la catégorie professionnelle et le type d'activité. Ses conclusions sont résumées dans le tableau suivant:

Matières sur lesquelles doit porter recyclage

| CATEGORIES PROFESSIONNELLES | ACTIVITES | | | | | | |
|---|---|---|---|---|---|---|---|
| | A Recherche fonda-mentale | B Recherche appliquée | C Etudes de systèmes | D Etudes techniques des produits | E Pro-duction | F Gestion admi-nistrative | G Vente |
| Cadres de direction | ●— Sciences fondamentales —● | | | | | | |
| | | ●———— connaissances specifiques liees à la fonction ————● | | | | | |
| | ●—————— techniques de gestion ————● | | | | | | |
| | ●—————— matières annexes ———● | | | | | | |
| | | | | | ●——● langues | | |
| Cadres superieurs | ●—Sciences fondamentales● | | | | | | |
| | | ●————connaissances specifiques liées à la fonction————● | | | | | |
| | ●—————— techniques de gestion ——● | | | | | | |
| | | | | | | probabilité statistique | |
| | ●—————— matières annexes ———● | | | | | | |
| | ●——— langues ———● | | | | | | |
| Cadres d'éxécution ingénieurs et cadres | ●——— connaissances spécifiques liees à la fonction ————● | | | | | | |
| | ●——— moyens d'expression——● | | | | | | |
| | ●————sciences fondamentales ——● | | | | | | |
| | ●——— matières annexes ——● | | | | | | |
| | ●——— langues ——● | | | | | | |
| | | | | | introduction ●——● à l'électro-nique | | formation générale ● |
| Techniciens supérieurs | ●——— connaissances spécifiques liées à la fonction ———● | | | | | | |
| | ●——— moyens d'expression ——● | | | | | | |
| | ●——— sciences fondamentales ——● | | | | | | |
| | ●—— matières annexes ——● | | | | | | |
| | ●——— langues ——● | | | | | | |
| | ●———formation générale ————● | | | | | | |
| Techniciens de production | ●— connaissances spécifiques liées à la fonction —● | | | | | | |
| | ●————perfectionnement —niveau B.E.I.——● | | | | | | |
| | ●———— matières annexes ——● | | | | | | |
| | ●——sciences fondamenthles ——● | | | | | | |
| | ●——— langues ——● | | | | | | |
| | ●——— formation générale ———● | | | | | | |

On voit ainsi, par exemple, que pour les cadres de direction engagés dans des activités de recherche et de conception, la formation complémentaire doit porter sur les sciences fondamentales.

e) L'étude américaine donne quatre causes qui expliquent l'obsolescence:
—l'accroissement des connaissances scientifiques et techniques,
—le retard des programmes de formation initiale par rapport aux découvertes scientifiques;
—l'utilisation généralisée des ordinateurs dans la solution de problèmes *scientifiques* et techniques;
—la pratique consistant à confier au personnel, pendant de longues périodes, des tâches très qualifiées.

L'étude française, qui couvre l'ensemble des besoins de formation en cours de carrière, donne à celle-ci les cinq objectifs suivants:
—préparation aux fonctions,
—adaptation aux fonctions supérieures,
—perfectionnement et remise à jour,
—promotion du travail
—reconversion des chômeurs,
—meilleure utilisation du personnel sous-utilisé.

f) L'étude américaine signale l'absence d'un système d'appréciation des services du PHQ suffisamment précis pour permettre d'établir une corrélation entre la qualité des services rendus et le degre d'obsolescence, et préconise des recherches approfondies dans ce domaine.

L'étude française ne parle pas de cette question.

Pour résumer, on peut dire que l'étude américaine, grâce à la plus grande variété d'activités industrielles couvertes éclaire davantage le problème de l'obsolescence dans l'industrie, mais cet éclairage est de caractère purement indicatif puisqu'il s'agit d'une étude pilote non représentative. L'étude française donne des indications assez précises pour une industrie déterminée et cherche à en dégager une méthode d'analyse qui n'a pas été appliquée à notre connaissance. Ce qu'il faut retenir de ces deux études, qui sont les meilleures dans leur genre à l'heure actuelle, c'est que nous sommes encore extrêment loin de connaître le phénomène de l'inadaptation et les mesures nécessaires pour la combattre. Le fait que les deux études aient été commandées par les pouvoirs publics révèle cependant la préoccupation de ces derniers pour un problème dont l'existence n'est pas mise en doute et qui demande une solution urgente.

### Etude couvrant l'ensemble de l'industrie d'un pays

Cette étude a été menée en Italie par le groupe italien créé à la suite d'une recommandation de l'O.C.D.E. pour étudier les problèmes qui se posent à la charnière de l'éducation et de l'emploi. Elle a fait l'objet d'un contrat passé entre l'O.C.D.E. et le Ministère italien de l'Education Nationale. Contrairement aux études mentionnées précédement, elle couvre l'ensemble de l'industrie italienne. Cependant, seules les entreprises employant plus de 500 personnes ont été couvertes, à l'exception de quelques entreprises à effectif moindre, mais employant des techniques de pointe dans un secteur à fort investissement en capital. L'enquête a été effectuée par questionnaire et interviews et a porté sur les mesures prises durant les 2 ou 3 années passées en matière de formation en cours de carrière du personnel de haute qualification. On remarquera donc que le problème important mais difficile de la détermination des besoins a été mis de côté au profit d'une enquête destinée à dresser un tableau des initiatives effectivement prises. Ces initiatives ont été classées sous 4 rubriques selon l'objectif visé par la formation:
a) insertion des cadres nouvellement engagés dans l'entreprise,
b) mise à jour des connaissances fondamentales,
c) complément de formation dans des spécialités déterminées,
d) reconversion à des fonctions nouvelles.

530 entreprises, soit 76% de celles qui emploient plus de 500 personnes, ont été touchées par l'enquête, mais seulement 191 d'entre elles, soit 36% ont répondu. Parmi celles qui ont répondu 101 entreprises (soit 53% des réponses) font état de mesures de formation systématiques prises pour accroître la qualification de leur personnel.

Il est certain, que ces 101 entreprises ne sont pas les seules où le personnel bénéficie d'une formation sur les lieux de travail. Mais il s'agit alors d'une formation diffuse, quasi spontanée, qui ne fait l'objet d'aucun programme, mais dont l'importance ne doit pas être négligée, compte tenu du tempérament italien trés imaginatif et créateur et porté vers la discussion et les échanges d'idées.

Quoi qu'il en soit, pour s'en tenir aux entreprises ayant un programme de formation officiel, elles ne représentent, par rapport à l'ensemble des entreprises employant plus de 500 personnes, qu'une proportion de 14% employant 17% du personnel dans l'industrie italienne.

Ce pourcentage global n'est pas très significatif, car la participation des entreprises varie considérablement selon les branches auxquelles elles appartiennent. Ainsi, dans la branche du caoutchouc et des plastiques, les entreprises qui ont un programme de formation représentent 80% des employés de cette industrie. Ce pourcentage descend à 40% des entreprises pour le pétrole, et à 34% dans les industries électriques et mécaniques, pour atteindre à peine quelques % dans les industries traditionnelles comme les textiles et les cuirs, où la formation 'diffuse,' qui est traditionnelle, est dominante. D.une manière générale, plus on se trouve dans un secteur à technique avancée et plus l'entreprise est grande, plus les efforts de formation sont systématiques et intenses:

*Pourcentage des entreprises ayant répondu à l'enquête et possédant un programme de formation officiel*

| Nombre d'employés | Ont répondu nombre | Possèdent un programme de formation | % |
|---|---|---|---|
| 500 − 2000 | 135 | 60 | 44 |
| 2000 − 5000 | 34 | 21 | 61 |
| 5000 − 10000 | 12 | 10 | 83 |
| Plus de 10 000 | 10 | 10 | 100 |

**Modalités de la formation**

L'enquête a permis de distinguer la formation à l'intérieur de l'entreprise (systém-atique ou non) et celle donnée à l'extérieur.

La *formation systématique* à l'intérieur des entreprises est le fait des grandes entreprises qui possèdent un service spécialisé et un nombreux personnel auquel sont offerts des programmes diversifiés. Ces programmes sont étudiés en général en vue du développement des carrières, avec le souci d'améliorer les capacités d'un individu pour lui permettre de bien remplir ses fonctions présentes et le préparer à ses fonctions futures.

*Formation non systématique*: il y a des entreprises où la formation n'est donnée d'une manière systématique, mais où le souci en existe à l'état latent. Il est très difficile d'évaluer l'efficacité de cette formation non systématique qui peut, grâce à la souplesse qu'elle possède, avoir une grande efficacitè.

*Formation à l'extérieur des entreprises*: il s'agit de la formation donnée dans le cadre de l'Université ou dans des centres créés par des associations diverses, des conceils en organisation, des instituts spécialisés offrant des cours de caractère spécifique et de courte durée. Parmi les 101 entreprises qui ont répondu, la moitié ont recours aux services de ces institutions pour la mise à jour des connaissances (33) et pour un complément de formation (46). Les cadres qui y sont envoyés sont en général, ceux qui possèdent une certaine expérience professionnelle et une excellente connaissance de l'entreprise.

## Modalités de la formation selon l'objetif visé

En ce qui concerne l'*insertion*, les 101 entreprises qui ont répondu qu'elles avaient un programme bien défini, se répartissent comme suit:
Programme formel:  37 entreprises dont 28 ont des cours internes bien organisès.
Apprentissage traditionnel méthodique: 34 entreprises
Rotation de postes: 29 entreprises,
Programme externe: 2 entreprises.

En ce qui concerne le *complément de formation*, la répartition est la suivante:
Programme interne: 54 entreprises
Programme externe: 33 entreprises
Apprentissage traditionnel méthodique: 29 entreprises.

Pour la *remise à jour des connaissances*, les entreprises se répartissent comme suit:
Programme interne: 39
Programme externe: 46
Lectures dirigées: 31.

Notons que pour la remise à jour les cours externes sont plus fréquents que pour le complément de formation technique spécialisée que l'entreprise est parfois seule à donner.

Pour la *reconversion*, seules 17 entreprises sur les 101 ont répondu, d'une manière d'ailleurs assez vague, car l'idée déterminante semble être qu'il s'agit là d'une responsabilité qui dépasse les entreprises et devrait être assumée par la société tout entière.

## Formation et carrière

L'enquête a permis de mettre en lumière que l'importance qu'attachent les airecteurs et chefs d'entreprises aux activités de formation est très variable. Dans les entreprises où les activités sont reliées à la politique de personnel, elles sont l'objet d'une attention particulière de la part des autorités les plus élevées. Dans les autres, elles constituent souvent une activité mineure.

## Contenu des programmes de formation

Seulps une vingtaine d'entreprises ont fourni des renseignement sur les matières enseignées, la durée des cours, la désignation des stagiaires, etc. On remarque d'abord qu'il n'y a pas toujours une distinction très nette entre certains cours destinés à faciliter l'insertion des jeunes diplômés et ceux qui ont pour but de donner un complément de formation au personnel existant.

D'autre part, ces cours sont très spécifiques et se rapportent directement aux activités de l'entreprise; leur contenu varie donc considérablement d'une entreprise à l'autre.

Les méthodes de formation utilisées restent traditionnelles: cours magistraux, exercices pratiques, utilisation d'aides audio-visuelles. Certaines entreprises signalent des méthodes 'actives': discussions en petits groupes, projets, etc.

### Coût de la formation

L'enquête italienne a enfin cherché à déterminer le coût de la formation donnée par les entreprises à leurs agents de haute qualification. L'évaluation a porté sur les dépenses directes en argent correspondant aux droits d'inscription à des cours extérieurs, aux frais de déplacement pour participer à des congrés ou à des réunions, et sur les dépenses que représente le temps passé par les agents de l'entreprise pendant lequel les salaires sont versés. Seules 54 entreprises sur le 101 ont donné des renseignements sur les coûts. Il s'agit des plus grandes entreprises représentant un effectif de 475,000 employés dont 56,000 diplômés. Le coût moyen de la formation par entreprise pour l'année 1967 s'élève à 209 millions de lires, mais il y a des variations considérables selon la taille et les secteurs.

*Coût moyen par entreprise selon le nombre d'employés*

| de 500 à 2 000 diplômés | 11,– |
|---|---|
| de 2 000 à 5 000 diplômés | 179,1 |
| de 5 000 à 10 000 diplômés | 54,4 |
| plus de 10 000 diplômés | 978,1 |
| Total | 208,8 |

*Coût moyen par entreprise selon le secteur économique*

| Industrie alimentaire | 27,– |
|---|---|
| ”       textile | 21,7 |
| ”       de l'habillement | 8,– |
| ”       des papiers et cartons | 32,4 |
| ”       du caoutchouc, plastique, textiles artificiel et synthétique | 432,1 |
| ”       chimique | 177,8 |
| ”       produits du pétrole | 171,9 |
| ”       métallurgie | 175,1 |
| ”       mécanique | 604,8 |
| ”       électromécanique | 257,4 |
| Total des industries de transformation | 214,1 |
| Transport et communications, eau, gaz, électricité | 124,8 |
| Total général | 208,8 |

Pour 41 des entreprises enquêtées, l'étude a réussi a rapporter le coût au chiffre d'affaire de l'entreprise. Là encore il y a des variations autour d'une moyenne de 0, 18%.

*Pourcentage de coût de la formation par rapport au chiffre d'affaires*

| | |
|---|---|
| *Selon la taille de l'entreprise:* | |
| de 500 à 2 000 employés | 0,04 % |
| de 2 000 à 5 000 employés | 0,15 % |
| de 5 000 à 10 000 employés | 0,09 % |
| plus de 10 000 employés | 0,24 % |
| Total | 0,18 % |
| | |
| *Selon la secteur économique:* | |
| Industrie alimentaire | 0,09 % |
| ''        textile | 0,14 % |
| ''        des papiers et cartons | 0,12 % |
| ''        textiles artificiels et synthétiques | 0,16 % |
| ''        chimique | 0,10 % |
| ''        des produits du pétroles | 0,06 % |
| ''        métallurgique | 0,14 % |
| ''        mécanique | 0,28 % |
| ''        électromécanique | 0,80 % |
| Total pour les industrie de transformation | 0,19 % |
| | |
| Transport, communications, eau, gaz et électricité | 0,09 % |
| Total général | 0,18 % |

Si l'on considère les entreprises individuelles, les variations sont extrêment grandes et dépendent non seulement de la taille et du secteur d'activité, mais de la plus ou moins grande détermination des chefs d'entreprise à mettre en oeuvre des techniques avancées. Dans certaines entreprises le pourcentage du chiffre d'affaire consacré à la formation n'est que de 0,01%. A l'autre extrémité, on trouve une entreprise où il est de 1,28 et deux qui dépassent 0,50%.

Il faut noter l'effort relativement faible des entreprises de 5,000 à 10,000 employées qui peut être attribué soit au fait que la proportion des diplômés y est moindre, soit que leur taille est encore insuffisante pour leur permettre de mettre en oeuvre un programme de modernisation très dynamique.

## ROLE DES POUVOIRS PUBLICS

Il n'existe guère de pays, quel qu'en soit le régime politique où le gouvernement ne se sente responsable à un degré plus ou moins grand, du développement économique. Dans le cas qui nous occupe, et en raison aussi, comme on l'a indiqué, des incidences sociales de l'inadaptation, la nécessité de doter chaque citoyen d'une qualification lui permettant de remplir un rôle productif dans l'économie tout en se réalisant pleinement sur le plan personnel a déjà conduit certains pays à prendre des mesures importantes concrétisées par des lois. A titre d'exemple, nous considérerons les cas du Royaume-Uni et de la France.

Il existe entre les lois française et anglaise une très grande analogie d'objectifs, mais des différences notables en ce qui concerne la structure, l'organisation et le mode de fonctionnement des organismes responsables, ainsi que les compétences de ces organismes.

La loi anglaise du 12 mars 1964 s'intitule 'Loi relative à la formation professionnelle dans l'industrie'; le titre de la loi françcaise du 3 décembre 1966 est 'Loi d'orientation et de programme sur la formation professionnelle.' Cette loi a été complétée par la loi du 31 décembre 1968 relative à la rémunération des stagiaires de la formation professionnelle.

## 1. Objectifs

Ces lois visent toutes deux trois objectifs principaux:
—assurer à l'économie un effectif suffisant de travailleurs qualifiés à touts les niveaux;
—amèliorer la qualité et l'efficacité de la formation;
—répartir équitablement le coût de la formation entre tous les intéressés.

Cependant la loi française vise explicitement à favoriser l'accès à la culture aussi bien qu'à la qualification professionnelle alors que la loi anglaise ne mentionne que la formation en vue des emplois dans l'industrie et le commerce. Cette différence s'explique par le fait qu'il existe en Angleterre un système d'"éducation continue" (further education) où peuvent continuer à se cultiver ceux qui ont dépassé l'âge de la scolarité obligatoire.

## 2. Domaine d'application

La loi anglaise intéresse les activités économiques seules: industrie, agriculture, commerce, finances, transports, etc.

La loi française, en plus des activités économiques, comprend des dispositions applicables à la fonction publique. De plus, en ce qui concerne une catégorie particulière de travailleurs, les cadres de direction et de gestion, elle prévoit la création d'un organisme spécial, la fondation nationale pour l'enseignement de la gestion des entreprises.

## 3. Instances responsables au niveau national

S'agissant de problèmes qui intéressent les responsables des différents aspects de l'activité économique et ceux de l'éducation, il est naturel que plusieurs administrations et organisation aient un rôle à jouer dans l'application de ces lois. Cependant, la loi anglaise donne au Ministre du Travail (actuellement Ministre de l'emploi et de la productivité) un rôle prédominant, ce qui n'exclut pas des responsabilités très précises confiées aux autorités responsables de l'enseignement.

En France, la responsabilité essentielle appartient au Premier Ministre secondé par le Ministre de l'Education nationale qui semble devoir jouer un rôle important.

Dans les deux pays, il existe un organisme au niveau national chargé des problèmes généraux concernant l'application de la loi et des recherches nécessaires à éclairer les instances responsables. Toutefois la composition et les règles de fonctionnement de ces organismes sont différentes.

Au Royaume-Uni, un Conseil central de la formation professionnelle est chargé de conseiller le Ministre sur l'application de la loi et de le tenir au courant de son exécution. Il comprend, sous la présidence d'une personnalité indépendante: 6 représentants des employeurs, 6 représentants des travailleurs, 2 des industries nationalisées, 3 présidents de Conseil de formation dans l'industrie, 6 délégués des services d'éducation et des collèges techniques sur avis du Ministre de l'éducation, et 6 membres indépendants ayant une grande activité dans le domaine de l'enseignement technique et de la formation dans l'industrie. Des fonctionnaires du Ministère du Travail et du Ministère de l'Education et de la Science assistent aux réunions. Ce conseil est aidé par un nombre de Comités spéciaux tels que: Comité de politique générale, Comité commercial et administratif, Comité de la recherche, Comité écossais, Comité Gallois, etc.

En France, la structure administrative est beaucoup plus complexe: un 'Comité interministériel,' présidé par le Premier Ministre, et dont le vice-président est le Ministre de l'Education nationale, constitue l'organe d'exécution sur le plan national, assisté dans ses travaux par un 'groupe permanent des hauts fonctionnaires' et un Conseil de gestion du fonds de la formation professionnelle. Un 'Conseil National de la formation professionnelle, de la promotion sociale et de l'emploi' réunissant des représentants des pouvoirs publics, des organisations d'employeurs et des syndicats de salariés, constitue l'organe consultatif. Il donne son avis sur les orientations de la politique de formation professionnelle et de promotion sociale en fonction des besoins de l'économie, suggère les mesures propres à assurer une meilleure coopération entre les administrations et les organisations d'employeurs et d'employés et formule des propositions en vue d'une meilleure adaptation des programmes et des méthodes aux besoins des différentes catégories de personnel.

### 4. Organes décentralisés

Une grande différence apparaît dans les modalités de démultiplication des activités.

Au Royaume-Uni, la démultiplication est réalisée sur le plan des professions. Chaque profession possède un 'Conseil de formation professionnelle' crée par le Ministre de l'emploi et de la productivité, après consultation des responsables des travailleurs et des employeurs de l'activité économique considérée et sur avis du Secrétaire d'Etat à l'Education et à la Science et du Secrétaire d'Etat pour l'Ecosse. Chaque conseil comprend, sous la présidence d'une personnalité provenant de la profession, un professeur de l'enseignement technique et un fonctionnaire d'une administration scolaire locale [1]. Le nombre des membres n'est pas défini par la loi et peut varier d'un secteur à l'autre. Le nombre des conseils n'est pas non plus précisé, mais on estime qu'il faudrait au total une trentaine de conseils pour couvrir l'ensemble des activités économiques du pays[2]. Un conseil peut d'ailleurs être responsable pour une seule industrie ou pour un groupe d'industries connexes. Inversement, une entreprise peut être rattachée à deux Conseils différents pour la formation de son personnel de différentes spécialités.

---

[1] Les responsabilités éducatives au Royaume-Uni ne sont pas centralisées entre

En France, la démultiplication des actions est fondée sur la *répartition géographique*: dans chaque région est institué un Comité régional qui est le reflet, à l'échelon régional, du comité national de la formation professionnelle, de la promotion sociale et de l'emploi. La responsabilité exécutive appartient au Préfet des régions assisté par le groupe régional des hauts fonctionnaires.

## 5. Compétence et fonctionnement

Il existe également une différence très notable entre la compétence et les règles de fonctionnement des Comités de formation au Royaume-Uni et les Comités régionaux de la formation professionnelle, de la promotion sociale et de l'emploi en France. Le rôle essentiel des conseils de formation en Angleterre est de s'assurer qu'un nombre suffisant de travailleurs de tous niveaux reçoive une formation adéquate. Ils étudient à cet effet les types de qualification nécessaires aux différents niveaux du personnel employé dans leur industrie et publient des recommandations sur la nature et la durée de la formation, ainsi que sur l'enseignement post-scolaire[3] que les intéressés devraient suivre.

Ils n'imposent aux entreprises aucune obligation et se bornent à accorder aux entreprises qui ont des programmes de formation, des subventions proportionnelles à l'importance de ces activités (nombre de personnes formées, durée des cours, niveau, etc.), après s'être assurés que les normes prescrites, ont été observées.

Les conseils ont également pour responsabilité de se procurer les ressources nécessaires pour la réalisation des programmes qu'ils préconisent, et ont à cet effet, le droit d'imposer une taxe aux entreprises, sous réserve de l'accord du Ministre qui en informe le Parlement.

En France, les Comités régionaux, échelon décentralisé du Comité national, ne sont, comme on l'a vu, que des organes consultatifs. L'exécution de la loi appartient aux Préfets régionaux, subordonnés hiérarchiques des Ministres. Le but de leur action est de faire naitre des initiatives en matière de formation professionnelle en offrant des 'conventions' aux centres déjà existants ou nouvellement créés. La convention est un contrat négocié entre l'Etat, représenté par le Minstre compétent pour l'activité considérée et l'organisme de formation. L'Etat joue ainsi un rôle de catalyseur et de stimulant en fonction des besoins de l'économie et cherche à associer aux activités de formation les entreprises, les associations professionnelles, les syndicats, les collecti-vités locales dont l'action doit compléter celle des écoles et des universités. Pour bénéficier d'une convention, le centre bénéficiaire d'une convention doit offrir une formation tenant compte à la fois des besoins conjoncturels et des perspectives à long terme, c'est à dire:
a) des actions en faveur des jeunes sortant de l'école,
b) des actions en faveur des travailleurs en activité,
c) des actions de promotion sociale.

---

les mains du Ministre de l'Education comme en France. Elles sont exercées par les différentes "autorités d'éducation" locales dont le nombre atteint 163.

[2] Le rapport annuel pour 1969 indique que le nombre de conseils déjà consitués est de 28.

[3] Il s'agit de l'enseignment dispensé sous le nom de 'Further Education.'

La loi de 1968 énumère les différents types de stages (conversion, adaptation, promotion professionnelle, préformation, actualisation des connaissances, etc.) et prévoit la possibilité par les stagiaires de recevoir une rénumération calculée en fonction du salaire qu'ils percevaient avant leur stage.

## 6. Financement

Il existe également des différences notables dans le système de financement. En France, la loi de 1966 a voulu traiter toutes les entreprises d'une manière uniforme. Elle impose une taxe unique de 0,6% de l'ensemble des salaires payés par chaque entreprise, quelle que soit sa taille ou sa branche d'activité.

Au Royaume-Uni, le taux d'imposition varie selon l'industrie considérée et, ainsi qu'on l'a vu plus haut, c'est le Conseil de formation compétent pour cette industrie qui le fixe. C'est ce qui explique une très grande diversité dans les taux qui vont de 0,55% de l'ensemble des salaires payés dans l'industrie de la construction navale à 2,5% dans l'industrie mécanique et électrique.

Dans les deux pays, en plus de la contribution de l'industrie, il est prévu que l'Etat pourra verser des subventions pour l'exécution des programmes de formation.

En France, la loi prévoit la création auprès du Premier Ministre d'un 'fonds de la formation professionnelle et de la promotion sociale' alimenté d'une part par la taxe d'apprentissage, et d'autre part par une dotation budgétaire annuelle égale au moins au produit de cette taxe.

Au Royaume-Uni, l'Etat peut accorder des subventions et des prêts dont le montant n'est pas déterminé; il dépend d'une négociation entre le Conseil de formation intéressé; et le Ministre de l'emploi et de la productivité.

Il existe également une différence dans les modalités d'application de ces dispositions financières: en France, les entreprises qui ont un programme de formation peuvent obtenir l'autorisation de déduire leurs dépenses de formation de la taxe qu'elles doivent au Trésor. Au Royaume-Uni, toutes les entreprises versent la taxe et sont ensuite remboursées au prorata des dépenses de formation qu'elles ont faites. Ce système a pour résultat une répartition plus équitable des dépenses car une entreprise anglaise peut recevoir des subventions dépassant le montant de la taxe qu'elle a versée, si elle se trouve avoir donné suffisamment de formation pour justifier un tel montant. En France, au contraire, l'entreprise qui a un programme de formation qui lui coute plus que la taxe d'apprentissage dont elle serait redevable, ne peut tout au plus espérer obtenir que la dispense totale de cette taxe.

## 7. Effet produit par ces lois sur la formation du capital de qualifications

Les informations nous manquent ici, mais seront complétées au cours de l'exposé lorsque le bilan que les pays doivent fournir à l'O.C.D.E. nous seront parvenus.

## CONCLUSIONS

Sous l'étiquette d'obsolescence, le phénomène auquel on assiste est, en fait, celui du manque d'adaptabilité aux conditions changeantes de l'économie et de la société. Les progrès des sciences et des techniques ont une part importante dans ce phénomène non seulement parce que les connaissances professionnelles du personnel se trouvent dépassées, mais aussi, pour une grande part, en raison des changements intervenus dans les conditions de vie et de travail dans des domaines étrangers à leur spécialité.

Il se produit ainsi une sorte de course-poursuite entre les besoins de l'économie et les qualifications possédées par les travailleurs de toute catégorie qui donne naissance à une sensation de malaise en raison de la confusion qui règne dans les esprits sur la notion de besoin de l'économie et les motifs véritables qui expliquent qu'un poste donné se trouve confié à un individu déterminé (quelle est la part du 'besoin' économique objectif dans une telle nomination? ) et de l'effort important d'adaptation demandé à chacun sans qu'il en perçoive clairement l'utilité: cet effort en effet, lui est demandé en général trop tard et se présente comme une mesure isolée destinée à faire face à une situation de crise, car les politiques de personnel sont encore bien imparfaites dans beaucoup de cas.

Combattre l'obsolescence, c'est mener des actions visant à rendre le personnel de tous les niveaux aptes à faire face ses responsabilités à chaque instant. Il s'agit donc de l'essence même de toute politique de main-d'oeuvre qui comporte, en particulier, un ensemb le de mesures de formation.

Précisions que la formation en cours de carrière commence dès l'instant où l'individu entre dans la vie professionnelle: quelles que soient les réformes du système éducatif, celui-ci ne peut, et ne doit d'ailleurs pas, mettre sur le marché du travail des hommes préparés à des tâches prçises. Un des premiers rôles des employeurs, compris depuis longtemps par les meilleurs d'entre eux, consiste précisément à se préoccuper de la formation de leur personnel dès le début de leur carrière.

Toutefois, les entreprises qui ont pris conscience de ce rôle et qui ont la volonté et les moyens de le remplir n'occupent qu'un pourcentage relativement faible de travailleurs. C'est la raison pour laquelle, tant pour prévenir le malaise signalé plus haut et l'agitation sociale qui peut en être la conséquence, que pour doter l'économie nationale en personnel qualifié, les gouvernements ont été amenés à intervenir par des mesures s'appliquant à l'ensemble des travailleurs.

Dans cette action, ainsi qu'on l'a vu, les gouvernements semblent être pris de court: la pression des nécessités les oblige à agir alors que les information leur manquent pour fonder une action véritablement éclairée. A cet égard, les recherches dont on a donné quelques exemples peuvent être considérées comme un utile commencement mais beaucoup reste encore à faire et les pouvoirs publics, dans les pays Membres, en ont nettement pris conscience.

On décèle ainsi une tendance à développer les études et recherches, ce que l'OCDE cherche de son côté à encourager en offrant des contrats à certains pays Membres et à accroître l'intervention des pouvoirs publics par des mesures législatives.

Il est intéressant de citer, à ce dernier point de vue, la législation intervenue récemment en Allemagne: la loit sur la promotion de l'emploi dont l'application a commencé le 1er juillet 1969 et celle sur la formation professionnelle qui est entrée en vigueur le 1er septembre 1969 donnent toutes deux à l'Etat Fédéral la possibilite d'intervenir énergiquement par des actions visant à accroitre la qualification du personnel de tous niveaux, à le rendre apte à s'adapter à de nombreux emplois et à établir une collaboration encore plus intime entre le système scolaire et le monde économique pour la formation des hommes.

A ce titre la législation allemande correspond d'une manière directe au thème central que l'OCDE se propose de traiter au cours de sa conférence intergouvernementale sur l'utilisation du PHQ de 1971 à savoir: la responsabilité conjointe des milieux éducatifs et économiques dans la formation des hommes.

## REFERENCES

1. Fayol, Henri *Administration industriel et générale*. Paris: Dunod.
2. Norgren, Paul H. and Warner, Aaron W. *Obsolescence and Updating of Engineers' and Scientists' Skills*. Office of Manpower Policy, Evaluation and Research, US Dept. of Labor.
3. Secrétariat Générale du Comité Interministériel de la Formation Professionnelle et de la Promotion Sociale *Le Recyclage des Cadres et Techniciens dans les Industries de Pointe* 1968.

# Motivational Factors in Professional Updating

S. S. Dubin    The Pennsylvania State University

The accelerating pace of information growth, the increasing complexity of scientific technology, and the changes in educational, managerial, social, economic and political institutions have created conditions of unprecedented flux in man's environment. It is becoming increasingly difficult for persons in the skilled professions to keep abreast of current developments, to keep from being inundated by new knowledge. But the plight of the professional, especially the scientist or the technologist, is the more severe because he is working with ideas and materials which are most subject to rapid change and obsolescence. Dr. James Killian, formerly president of the Massachusetts Institute of Technology, has pegged the half-life of an engineer's usefulness at about seven and one-half years. He interprets this to mean that the engineer is only half as valuable technically to a firm seven and one-half years after graduation as he was the day he received his degreee.

## BRIEF REVIEW OF THE LITERATURE

Research on this type of obsolescence is relatively new; the literature is not extensive. It may be appropriate at the outset to review some of the more descriptive studies in the field. In 1963, the Organization for Economic Co-operation and Development (OECD) published a study which reported the number of highly qualified scientists and engineers available in OECD countries, the extent of their employment in industry, teaching, and administration, and the need and demand for qualified manpower for the purpose of maintaining or accelerating the rate of economic growth (OECD, 1963). A subsequent conference examined policies required for updating the educational system to provide training for economic needs, and means by which industry and government could optimize the use of highly qualified personnel by in-career training (OECD, 1967).

The success of Sputnik in 1957, which demonstrated Russian engineering expertise, resulted in a drastic revision of engineering curricula in the United States. The new curricula took care of current engineering students. But what was to be done about the thousands of engineers who had graduated prior to 1957 and who had been out of college for five, ten or twenty-five years? Dean Gordon S. Brown (1963) of the Massachusetts Institute of Technology estimated that nearly half of all the bachelor's degrees in engineering were granted before 1953, prior to the time when engineering curricula began to take on a stronger scientific base. Between 1940 and 1962, approximately 600,000 engineers were graduated from the engineering colleges with a bachelor's degree, 93,000 with a master's degree and 10,000 with a Ph.D. degree. Lord Jackson described the magnitude of the obsolescence problem in the United Kingdom in another paper in this symposium.

In 1963, research was initiated at The Pennsylvania State University to determine what new areas of knowledge were needed by engineers who had been out of school for a number of years. A series of studies was published based on a sample of 2,090 engineers by various specialties (electrical, aeronautical, mechanical, etc.) and by various industrial categories and sizes of organisations in the state of Pennsylvania (Dubin and Marlow, 1965a). The results provided data on the self-perceived educational needs pf engineers who had been out of college for at least five years in subject areas in which they needed retooling. This study also consituted a rationale for offering new courses in the skills and knowledge which engineers reported they needed most. Almost 40 changes were made in the curriculum of The Pennsylvania State University College of Engineering; new courses in probability and statistics and computer technology were introduced, and modifications were made in many of the existing courses.

The investigation concerning engineers was followed by studies of other professional groups: hospital supervisors (Dubin & Marlow, 1965b), managers (Dubin, Alderman & Marlow, 1967), municipal managers (Dubin, Alderman & Marlow, 1968), and, currently, natural resource managers and scientists (George & Dubin). In these studies the aim was to determine the self-perceived educational needs of respondents, their subordinates and superiors in scientific subject areas, the extent of their participation in continuing education, methods of updating preferred, motivation for updating, attitudes of supervisors towards development of subordinates, the availability of financial assistance, and reasons for not updating. In some of the studies an additional section dealt with self-development planning projected over a period of five years.

A division of the American Society of Engineering Education, known as the Engineering College Achievement Council and the Relations Within Industry Feedback Committee (ECAC-RWI), surveyed engineers to determine the subjects in which additional training was necessary (1965). In both the Penn State and ECAC-RWI studies the most frequently mentioned topics were management and communication skills, probability and statistics, and computer applications and mathematics.

The Goals Study Committee of the American Society of Engineering Education put forth a major statement of the new professional goals for the whole organization (1968). In the next year, the National Science Foundation in the United States published "Continuing Education for Research and Development Careers" (1969), a study which reported on the motivation of R & D scientists in maintaining their scientific competence and the views of top management on continuing education. R & D personnel see themselves as being on the foremost frontier of science and, according to this study, regard continuing education as a necessity in their professional obligation to keep up to date, not as a remedial process. They do not see themselves or their colleagues as obsolete or not obsolete. The study also disclosed that top management recognized its responsibility to provide opportunities for continuing education but expected the individual scientist or engineer to be self-motivated. The authors recommended that management should provide a supportive educational environment, allowing attendance at professional meetings, arranging and sponsoring in-lab lectures and seminars, and granting sabbatical leaves.

Margulies and Rala (1967) carried on interviews with scientists and engineers in advanced technology laboratories in the aerospace and nuclear fields from which they evolved five categories of activities important for professional growth.

A survey of post-doctoral training needs of industrial psychologists found that 70% of the respondents were interested in post-doctoral training, while 60% thought that the professional association had a responsibility for sponsoring such programs (Lawler, 1967). The study included questions about training experience taken within the past five years, the most valuable and least valuable past training, and the most needed areas of future training, and plans for satisfying these needs. Another example of awareness of updating needs by professional organizations is the survey conducted by the American Institute of Certified Public Accountants, which called attention to new skills needed by certified accountants to provide the public with up-to-date service (Roy & MacNeil, 1967).

Frederick C. Hass' study entitled "Executive Obsolescence" provided information on identifying and measuring obsolescence in executives in industry (1968).

## DEFINITIONS OF OBSOLESCENCE

At present no definition of obsolescence has complete acceptance or currency among workers in the field. It may be helpful to cite some attempts to describe the conditions of obsolescence as it refers to scientists, engineers and managers.

Theodore W. Ferdinand has described three types of obsolescence for the purpose of identifying the nature and causes of obsolescence among engineers and scientists: professional, areal, and ex-officio (1966). He asserted that remedial programs could be more effectively implemented once the type of obsolescence was determined. According to his definitions, professional obsolescence exists in those persons whose technical competence does not embrace the farthest reaches of knowledge and technique in their profession. Areal obsolescence refers to a lack of knowledge in the technical specialty of a person who has allowed himself to settle complacently into a narrow specialized area. Symptoms of areal obsolescence are generally found in persons who are "less likely to apply rigorous analysis and mathematical techniques to the solution of problems, who tend to substitute 'judgment' for scientific evaluation, who encounter increasing difficulty in reading technical papers, even in their own area, and who regard innovations with hostility." Obsolescent individuals tend to be afflicted with a complacency which prevents their anticipating or participating in radical developments about to unfold in their specialty. Ex-officio obsolescence is a form prevalent in scientists or technical persons assigned to administrative work. A common example is that of the engineer assigned to supervisory and administrative work who finds that his technical capablilites gradually decline and become outdated.

W. W. Siefert (1963) of the Massachusetts Institute of Technology arrived at a definition of obsolescence for engineering that has received wide acceptance: "the measurement at some point of time of the difference between the knowledge and skills possessed by a new graduate of a modern engineering curriculum and the knowledge and skills actually possessed by the practicing engineer who may have completed his formal education a number of years ago." Clifford Shumacher (1963) defined obsolescence as a "reduction in technical effectiveness resulting from a lack of knowledge of the new techniques and, what is more, perhaps entirely new technologies that have developed since the acquistion of the education by the individual."

A. Malmros (1963) divided obsolescence into two categories: rustiness which results from the lack of proper use; and failure to grow and keep up with changes. He associated the failure to grow and keep abreast of new developments with persistence of repetitive patterns of behaviour and the lack of sensitivity to change. He further identified five signs of obsolescence in engineers: (a) the engineer became less and less inclined to apply rigorous mathematical techniques to obtain solutions to his problems; (b) he encountered increasing difficulty in reading new technical papers and felt frustrated because he could not follow the mathematics; (c) new technical concepts were confusing to him; (d) new tasks and assignments began to look too difficult to be practical; and (e) contemporaries did not seek his advice.

Paul Norgren (1965) identified two major types of skill obsolescence: technology-based obsolescence and product-based obsolescence.

Walter Mahler (1965) defined managerial obsolescence as "the failure of the once capable manager to achieve results that are currently expected of him," He categorized several types of obsolescence: ability obsolescence—the manager's abilities and skills are no longer sufficient for him to keep up with past jobs; attitudinal obsolescence—the manager fails to maintain flexibility in attitude and approach, changing problems and conditions; creeping obsolescence—the nature of the job slowly changes and the incumbent slowly ossifies; and abrupt obsolescence—an innovation eliminates or drastically changes a manager's job. Burack and Pati (1970) stated that obsolescence occurs when innovation results in a discrepancy between job needs and managerial or professional capabilities.

Thomas Jacobs (1965) has described management obsolescence as the gap between the professional's conceptual development and both his conceptual assimilation and application ability.

Paul Mali (1970) recently developed an obsolescence index:

$$OI = \frac{\text{current knowledge understood by engineers}}{\text{current knowledge in the field}}$$

This equation is based on the rate of change versus time. A high rate of technological obsolescence is related to a high rate of growth. The curve which Mali developed is a conceptual one and shows that technological obsolescence is growing exponentially. The skills required to maintian and support these technologies lag. "It takes time for new knowledge to go through the process of being utilized and applied, and for the engineer to become aware of its existence. Thus there is a time lag. The big problem is that this lag is becoming broader and broader, wider and wider, as new technologies emerge. It is this lag which we refer to as 'technological obsolescence.' It is not forgetfulness, incapacity, or stupidity, nor is it the stagnancy of the mind. Simply it is the failure to keep abreast or current in the state of the art. It is the failure to achieve the results currently expected of an up-to-date engineer. It is the failure to advance with and at the same rate as the technological growth within the field. It is the failure to exploit the latest advances in the state of the art." Mali listed four causes of engineering obsolescence: (a) Failure to keep up with the change of knowledge in the field. In this sample 50% were unaware of new, emerging fields of knowledge according to the survey data. (b) A low level of utilization of technology in the field. Half of the participants admitted that their work assignments were essentially sub-professional. This results in skill atrophy. (c) Over-specialization. (d) Failure to plan a career. Many of the engineers did not do long-range planning for their careers and hence failed to avail themselves of opportunites for updating.

## A SYSTEMS MODEL FOR UPDATING

Updating is a learning process. The knowledge, information, techniques, methods and media accumulated by psychologists on the learning process are applicable to the process of updating. Only one of the conditions crucial to learning, namely motivation, will be considered in this paper.

The reverse of the activity of learning is the condition of obsolescence. Obsolescence is a decremental process comprising the loss of acquired knowledge and the non-acquisition of new learning which occurs unless effort is constantly made to repair the erosion of knowledge and to stimulate growth and innovation.

Applying present knowledge of learning and motivation to the maintenance of professional competence, how can professional persons be motivated to keep up-to-date? An emprical motivational model for updating based on a systems approach is illustrated in Figure 1 (Dubin & Cohen, 1970).

The motivation to update is a multi-dimensional process involving two large groups of variables: the individual and the environmental. Achievement motivation is the principal individual variable involved in this model. The environment or situational variables used in the model are: motivational aspects of supervisory behaviour, organizational climate, on-the-job problem solving, peer and group interaction, and management policy.

The input to this system is the individual. Box $W$ in the system represents the past formal education of the professional. Continuing into the main system, box $P$ represents the influence of supervision on possible updating. Next is box $A$ and $ta$, which are outside influences on the system caused by management policies. Box $I = B + K + D + E + F + Q$ represents various updating practices, such as on-the-job learning $(Q)$; taking courses $(F)$; reading $(E)$; training which occurs in organizations $(B)$; the learning which occurs during professional association meetings or publications of the professional associations $(K)$; and attendance at seminars and workshops $(D)$. A professional can go through any combination of $I$ simultaneously or one at a time. Boxes $G$ and $H$ represent the positive effects of group and peer interaction occurring on the job or within professional activity, and/or self-achievement as a result of the updating process. This is shown as feedback in this system. If no positive feedback occurs due to group interaction and/or self-achievement, the system can have a cycling effect back to the main system via the third feedback loop $(e)$. Finally, the output of this system is either an updated or an increasingly obsolete individual. Negative updating cannot occur in this system.

The mathematical equation of a professional updating system is shown in equation 1 below. This equation states that the updated professional is the result of many factors: past formal education, the extent of self-achievement and task orientation, the effects of supervisory behaviour, actuation of managerial policies which stimulate learning, peer group interaction, on-the-job learning and updating practices. Starting with summation point I, in Figure 1, it can be seen that $(t_{in}W + t_O)$ is multiplied by $P$. At summation point II, $[(t_{in}W + t_O) P + t_a A + t_O (G + H)]$ is multiplied by $I = B + K + D + E + F + Q$. This quantity is equal to $t_O$ (the ouput).

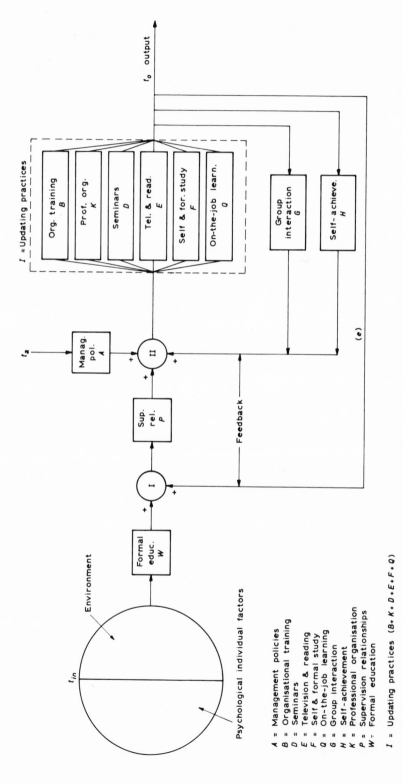

A = Management policies
B = Organisational training
D = Seminars
E = Television & reading
F = Self & formal study
Q = On-the-job learning
G = Group interaction
H = Self-achievement
K = Professional organisation
P = Supervision relationships
W = Formal education

I = Updating practices (B + K + D + E + F + Q)

Figure 1. A Model for professional updating of information.

Equation 1 below is the mathematical representation of the professional updating system described in Figure 1:

Equation 1:

$$t_O = \frac{I\,(WPt_{in} + t_a A)}{1 - I\,(G + H + P)}$$

| | | |
|---|---|---|
| $t_O$ | = | updated individual (output of system) |
| $t_{in}$ | = | individual coming into system(input) |
| $W$ | = | formal education |
| $P$ | = | supervision relationships |
| $A$ | = | management policies |
| $G$ | = | group interaction |
| $H$ | = | self-achievement |
| $t_a$ | = | actuation of management policies |
| $I$ | = | updating practices $(B + K + D + E + F + Q)$ |

It is planned that the model described in this paper be used as a device for determining the individual as well as group (company, etc.) factors which relate to professional updating when measuring instruments have been developed for each of the variables. It has potential as a diagnostic tool to determine where action should be taken to improve updating.

## MOTIVATIONAL DETERMINANTS FOR UPDATING

### Achievement Motivation

In this model, the principal individual determinant for updating is achievement motivation. Symbol H in the model represents the motivation to achieve. Achievement motivation, as described by Atkinson and Feather (1966), is an index of generalized motivation for achievement involving desire for success and fear of failure. Persons who are highly motivated are generally attracted to activities which require skill and excellence in performance. In terms of a theoretical model of motivation Vroom's (1964) expectancy theory provides a better understanding of updating behaviour because it incorporates motives like achievement, status, power, advancement, and self-actualization. Porter and Lawler (1968) utilized expectancy theory in a study of the relationship between managerial attitudes and job performance.

McClelland and Winters summarized the behavioral characteristics of achievement-oriented managers (1969). They found that high levels of achievement motivation are associated with entrepreneurial behavior, innovative risk-taking, and business success. Men with a high need to achieve tend to: seek and assume a high degree of personal responsibility; take moderate or calculated risks, set a challenging but realistic goals for themselves; develop comprehensive plans to help attain their goals; show preference for problem situations which provide concrete measurable feedback of their performance; seek out business opportunities where their desire to achieve will not be thwarted; spend time thinking about how to get things done better and take pride in accomplishment; and show more initiative and exploratory behavior by continually researching the environment to find tasks they can solve to their satisfaction. McClelland and Winters related achievement motivation to technological developments in various cultures and societies. They maintain that economic and technological growth necessitate judicious risk-taking and striving for successful performance.

Stringer advanced the position that a person's achievement behavior depends on his motives and his environment (1966). His motivation depends on three factors: the basic strength of the particular motive, the person's expectation that he can satisfy the motive in this situation, and the amount of satisfaction the person anticipates. He suggested the behaviors which should be taught to managers to stimulate achievement-motivated behavior: making responsibility and goals explicit; setting goals which call for a moderate degree of risk as opposed to extreme risk; adjusting specific goals so that a 50–50 chance of goal achievement always remains; rewarding managers for setting moderately risky goals as contrasted with safe goals—100% sure, providing prompt, unbiased feedback from superiors concerning managers' progress; emphasizing a climate of individual responsibility through coaching, and providing a climate of mutual support and encouragement.

Bass (1970) recently introduced the notion of task competence as a factor in job motivation. The task oriented person is described as being persistent, confident, objective, intelligent and single-minded. These qualities seem to be goal— and achievement-oriented and seem related to those who seek to keep themselves up-to-date.

### Motivational Aspects of Supervisory Behavior

One of the chief situational determinants for motivating to update is the attitude and behavior of the supervisor. In this context, we are not concerned with the whole gamut of supervisory behavior but only the motivational aspect.

Studies on engineers (Dubin & Marlow, 1965a) and managers (Dubin, Alderman & Marlow, 1967) have indicated that the supervisors are not developing their subordinates' professional growth. Sixty-four percent of 2,090 professional engineers reported that their supervisors took a noncommittal attitude towards their further education and developement. Similarly, 51% of 3,600 managers reported that their superiors are noncommittal about their further training. These findings suggest that supervisors are not using their subordinates' potential to the maximum. Corroboration of these findings was reported in the National Science Foundation Study: about one-third of the scientists and just under one-half of the engineers reported attitudes of non-interest on the part of their supervisors (1969).

Landis (1969) followed a similar course of inquiry with the question: "How does your immediate supervisor feel about further job-directed education or training?" Fifteen percent reported "very encouraging"; 47%, "somewhat encouraging"; and 37%, "not encouraging at all." He concluded that it is "the immediate supervisor that counts in the development of subordinates. If a boss does not encourage a man, he will not take further course work . . . unless the supervisor is willing to encourage and accommodate his men in spite of the possible interference with his work schedule, few men will undertake continuing studies."

Locke examined the role of the supervisor in facilitating subordinates' goal-setting activities as a means of enhancing employee commitment (1969). He pointed out that the supervisor aids in the motivational process by helping the subordinate to specify his goals within the context of his job and ensuring that the facilities exist for the subordinate to update his skills and to realize his goals. Thus the supervisor acts as a developer and facilitator of the subordinate's motivational potential rather than as a regulator, his traditional role.

The National Science Foundation Study provided further evidence of the key position of the supervisor (1969). Three types of supervisors were identified: the innovator, the administrator and the inactive supervisor. The innovative supervisor 'tries to create new opportunities in addition to existing ones, to provide novel and interesting ways for subordinates to undertake continuing education. The innovator is himself a stimulating and motivating element in the working environment. He is considerably more sensitive to the needs of his subordinates and is keenly perceptive of the resources available in the community. His enthusiasm for continuing education is such that he will contrive and create both stimulation and such other resources as specific workshops or courses or special seminars. He sees these techniques as ways to keep his staff on the frontiers of knowledge by incorporating the latest knowledge available into easily digestible and accessible forms.' The inactive supervisor is passive and noncommital in his attitudes. He conceives self-development as a responsibility of the employee apart from the working environment. He neither stimulates subordinates to pursue additional knowledge nor initiates continuing education on their behalf. The administrator conceives of his job as implementing organization policies and encouraging subordinates to use existing resources for self-development. The type of supervisor classified as administrator, innovator, or inactive determines the motivational level of subordinates.

Motivation can also be stimulated by supervisors through coaching. Coaching is a learning process which uses some fundamental principles of learning and development. In the coaching process, the subordinate should know what is expected of him, and the results he is to achieve; he should be given the opportunity to develop by being assigned tasks that challenge him, enable him to take risks and to explore the new areas of knowledge; he should be given feedback about how well he is doing, and he should be given guidance or assistance when needed, and rewarded or penalized on the basis of results.

Hinrichs described coaching as a direct expression of two basic employee development principles: (a) most employee development occurs on the job, and (b) personnel development must be a line-management responsibility (1966).

## Organizational Climate

Organizational climate as a means of determining group effectiveness in an organization is being given increased emphasis. In the current literature the variables which describe a motivating organizational climate usually include openness of communications, sensitivity and responsiveness to the individual's need for development, varied and challenging work assignments, opportunities for informal discussion and interaction with colleagues, recognition for successful work, opportunities to participate in decision making activities, responsibility in work assignments, and situations in which individuals may seek and find help.

Margulies and Raia (1967) interviewed R & D scientists and engineers on situational conditions which stimulated innovation. They concluded: 'When the organizational climate can be described as "open", with a high degree of experimentation, innovativeness and nurturance, the result is a "healthy" and highly creative organization—one in which individual motivation, and hence, individual activities contribute to the effective and efficient accomplishments of the organizational objectives. The nonadaptive organization, on the other hand, is insensitive to its environment. Individual motivation and creativity are suppressed, and the result is something less than the accomplishment of total organization objectives.'

Litwin and Stringer (1968) described a systematic theory of human motivation (McClelland-Atkinson) and suggested how it could be applied to the problems which managers encounter by means of the concept, organizational climate. The authors developed a number of devices to measure motivation and organizational climate. Their experimental field studies are representative of the application of motivation theory to organizational behavior by means of the environment variable, organizational climate. Litwin and Stringer identified four critical variables that managers must consider in dealing with motivational problems: the motives and needs the individual brings to a situation—achievement, power and affiliation; knowledge of the tasks that the manager must perform; the organizational climate that characterizes the work situation. Here the manager's leadership style is the critical determinant of organizational climate. Once the motivational problems are diagnosed as climate-based, then new skills need to be developed to change that climate; and the manager's personal strengths and limitations. In applying these motivational variables to actual conditions, the authors reported five action phases: 1) deciding what kind of climate is most appropriate (based on worker's needs and the job to be done); 2) assessing the present climate; 3) analyzing the climate gap and establishing a plan to reach the ideal climate; 4) taking concrete steps to improve climate; and 5) evaluating your effectiveness in terms of your action plan. (For a significant and original contribution to organizational climates which stimulate innovation of knowledge and skill, see Hesseling's chapter in this book.)

**On-the-Job Problem Solving**

Another important variable for motivating updating behavior is on-the-job learning or problem solving. Margulies and Raia (1967), investigating activities which are significant to professional growth, asked 290 R & D scientists and engineers: 'What was the most fruitful learning experience you have had over the past year or two?' The two most frequent responses were: on-the-job problem solving (42%), and interaction with colleagues (20%). The other activities were: publishing and independent reading (16%); formal courses (14%); and outside professional activities (4%). On-the-job problem solving was prevalent in organizations which provided stimulating work assignments described by responding engineers as 'interesting and diverse tasks'; 'broadening project'; and 'writing proposals which force me to dip into the literature and become current on everything connected with the project.' When on-the-job activities include challenging assignments, the exploration of new tasks enables the scientist and engineer to assess his own knowledge and fill in his gaps and deficiencies.

Pelz and Andrews reported some findings about scientists and engineers in job functions (in Allison's book, *The R & D Game, 1969*). The more kinds of research and development functions the scientists is engaged in, the better is his performance. Maximum performance seems to occur with four to five functions. To stimulate updating and build diversified skills in scientific personnel, Pelz and Andrews recommended: 'The next time you need to probe a specialized area, give the job to a man (or a small group) who is working in a related area. Don't give the job to a man who already is a specialist in that area. The man in a related specialty will dig into the field with new zest and excitement. He will develop fresh ideas that experts in the area would overlook.'

## Group and Peer Interaction

Interaction with colleagues on the job received the second highest proportion of responses (20%) in the Margulies and Raia (1967) study as sources of motivation and information-sharing necessary for professional learning. Building and maintaining informal relationships and networks of colleague interaction were seen as significant characteristics of good organizational environment. One person commented, 'It's tremendous when I get assigned to a project that forces me to work with people outside my own particular specialty, even outside my own discipline. It's very broadening and the exchange stimulates me to do a lot of reading.' On-the-job training in this context is a major source of continual learning.

## Management Policy

Many companies have educational assistance funds which reimburse employees who undertake continuing education courses, but few companies make continuous updating mandatory. In the Pennsylvania State University study (Dubin and Marlow, 1965a), 79% of engineers reported that their companies had educational assistance programs, showing the widespread availability of company payment for educational courses, but 74% of engineers reported that this availability had no effect in motivating them to undertake additional work. Similarly, 49% of middle managers (Dubin, Alderman & Marlow, 1967) said that company policy on financial aid had little effect on their decision to undertake further education. Evidence derived from these studies also indicated that taking additional course work was not sufficiently rewarded in industry and was not a requirement for promotion or salary increase. The availability of financial assistance for self improvement is obviously not a sufficient incentive for updating in employees.

Landis (1969) reported that engineers want immediate payoff from their continuing education in terms of recognition and salary. They are not willing to take course work for distant and uncertain future rewards. He concluded that most engineers are interested in performing better in the immediate, assigned job but few are challenged to make the extraordinary effort required to keep up with the latest developments in the profession.

Hughes and Wass (1970) described a company-installed mangement policy in which goal-oriented management behavior is rewarded by task satisfaction, financial rewards and goal accomplishment. The system provides a means for continuous updating of employees. Individual goal setting is integrated with the organization's goal setting. This is accomplished through the use of semiannual goal-oriented performance reviews in which each employee participates.

In these sessions, a great deal of importance is placed on identifying the individual's developmental needs, both present and future, to enable him to accomplish his specified goal.

Finally, it is interesting to note some practical measures for motivating professional persons to keep up to date which are being instituted. The French Atomic Energy Commission recently initiated the practice of declaring that scientific diplomas lapse after five years, unless revalidated by attendance at refresher courses and success in passing further examinations (Ford Foundation Report, 1966). The U. S. National

Advisory Commission on Health Manpower (1967) recommended that 'professional societies and state governments should explore the possibility of periodic relicensing of physicians and other health progressionals. Re-licensure should be granted either upon certification of acceptable performance in continuing education programs or upon the basis of challenge examinations in a practitioner's specialty.' Acting on this recommendation, the Oregon Medical Society (U.S.A.) in 1968 passed a regulation requiring physicians to continue their education in order to remain in good standard in the Association.

Professional obsolescence is now beginning to receive serious consideration by professional organizations and national policy making bodies.

## REFERENCES

Atkinson, John W. & Feather, Norman T. *A theory of achivement motivation.* New York: John Wiley & Sons, 1966.

American Society of Engineering Education. Goals of engineering education. *Jr. of Engineering Education,* Jan. 1968, 58 (5), 373-443.

Bass, B. M. The task of oriented manager. In B. M. Bass, R. Cooper & J. A. Hass (Ed.), *Managing for accomplishment.* Lexington, Massachusetts: Heath, 1970.

Brown, Gordon S. Closing the engineering gap: one approach. *Electrical Engineering,* July 1963.

Burach, E. H. & Pati, G. C. Technology and managerial obsolescence. *Michigan State University Business Topics,* Spring 1970, Vol. 18 #2, 49-56.

Dubin, Samuel S. & Marlow, H. LeRoy *A survey of continuing professional education for engineers in Pennnsylvania.* University Park, Pennsylvania. Continuing Education, The Pennsylvania State University, 1965a.

Dubin, Samuel S., & Marlow, H. LeRoy *The determination and measurement of supervisory training needs of hospital personnel.* University Park, Pennsylvania. Continuing Education, The Pennsylvania State University, 1965b.

Dubin, Samuel S., Alderman, Everett & Marlow, H. LeRoy *Managerial and supervisory educational needs of business and industry in Pennsylvania.* University Park, Pennsylvania: Continuing Education, The Pennsylvania State University, 1967.

Dubin, Samuel S., Alderman, Everett & Marlow, H. LeRoy *Education needs of managers and supervisors in cities, boroughs and townships in Pennsylvania.* University Park, Pennsylvania: Continuing Education, The Pennsylvania State University, 1968.

Dubin, S. S. & Cohen, D. Motivation to update from a systems approach. *Jr. of Engineering Education,* Jan. 1970, 366–368.

Engineering College Achievement Council and the Relations Within Industry Feedback Committee. Education in industry. *Jr. of Engineering Education,* May 1965, 254–256.

Ferdinand, Theodore N. On the obsolescence of scientists and engineers. *American Scientists,* 1966, 54 (1), 46–56.

Ford Foundation Report. Establishment of domestic satellite facilities by non-governmental entities. New York: Vol. 1, Nov. 1967.

George, John L. & Dubin, Samuel S. *The continuing professional education needs of natural resource managers and scientists.* University Park, Pennsylvania: Continuing Education, The Pennsylvania State University, 1971.

Hass, Frederick C. *Executive Obsolescence.* New York: American Management Association Research Study, 90, 1968.

Hinrichs, John R. *High-talent personnel.* New York: American Management Association, 1966.

Hughes, C. L. & Wass, D. L. Promoting goal seeking behaviour in managers In B. M. Bass, R. Cooper & J. A. Hass (Ed.), *Managing for accomplishment.* Lexington, Massachusetts: Heath, 1970. Pp. 102–108.

Jacobs, Thomas L. Combatting managerial obsolescence. *Business Horizons,* Oct. 1965, 58–60.

Landis, F. *Continuing engineering education–who really needs it?* Paper presented at Continuing Engineering Studies, American Society of Engineering Education, Pittsburgh, Pennsylvania, Nov. 5–7, 1969.

Lawler, Edward E. Post-doctoral training for industrial psychologists. *The Industrial Psychologist Newsletter,* 4 (2), Spring 1967, 34–40.

Litwin, George H. & Stringer, Robert A. *Motivation and organizational climate.* Boston, Massachusetts: Graduate School of Business Administration, Harvard University, 1968.

Locke, Edwin A. The supervisor as a motivator: his influence on goal setting. In B.M. Bass, R. Cooper & J. A. Hass (Ed.), *Managing for accomplishment.* Heath, 1970.

Mali, Paul Measurement of Obsolescence in engineering practices. *Continuing Education,* April 1970, 3 (2), 48–52.

Mahler, Walter R. Every company's problem–managerial obsolescence. *Personnel,* July–August, 1965, 8–10.

Malmros, A. *Obsolescence of engineering and scientific personnel in industry.* Paper presnted at Midwest Conference on Reducing Obsolescence of Engineering Skills, Illinois Institute of Technology, Chicago, 1963.

Margulies, Newton & Raia, Anthony P., Scentists, engineers and technological obsolescence. *California Management Review,* Winter, 1967, Vol. 10 (2), Pp. 43–48.

McClelland, David C. & Winter, David G. *Motivating Economic Achievement.* New York: Free Press, 1969.

National Advisory Commission on Health Manpower, Vol. 1, Nov. 1967.

National Science Foundatn. Continuing education for R & D careers. NSF 69–20, 1969.

Norgren, Paul *Pilot study of obsolescence of scientific and engineering skills.* New York: Columbia University, 1965.

Organization for Economic Co-operation and Development, Third international survey on the demand for and the supply of scientific and technical personnel. Paris, 1963.

Organization for Economic Co-operation and Development, Policy conference on highly qualified personnel. Paris, 1967

Pelz, D. C. & Andrews, F. M. Freedom in research (Ch. 4) & Diversity of Research (Ch. 5) In D. Allison (Ed.) *The R & D Game.* Cambridge, Massachusetts: MIT Press, 1969, Pp. 56–72.

Porter, Lyman W. & Lawler, Edward E. *Managerial attitudes and performance.* Homewood, Illinois: Irwin, 1968.

Roy, Robert H. & MacNeil, James H. *Horizons for a profession–the common body of knowledge for certified public accountants.* New York: American Institute of Certified Public Accountants, 1967.

Shumacher, Clifford H. *Reducing obsolescence of engineering skills.* Paper presented at Midwest Conference on Reducing Obsolescence of Engineering Skills, Institute of Technology, Chicago, 1963.

Siefert, W. W. *The prevention and cure of obsolescence in scientific and technical personnel.* Philadelphia: Industrial Research Institute, October, 1963.

Stringer, Robert A. Achievement motivation and management control. *Personnel Administration,* November–December, 1966, 3–16.

Vroom, V. H. *Work and Motivation.* New York: Wiley, 1964.

# Obsolescence as a Problem of Personal Initiative

William R. Dill    New York University

As a malady of individuals and organizations, obsolescence may be more unspellable than deadly. Its costs, however, are real and have proved difficult both to anticipate and to prevent. Conferences and seminars about the problem, unfortunately, often seem to be little more than gathering places for us to share our hypochondria about the disasters that lie ahead if we cannot find an appropriate vaccine or cure for the disease. Research that will help us build a better technology for guiding adult learning and self-renewal is still all too modest in scope. Of the new aids which entrepreneurs in education and business are selling to promote renewal and human growth, too many rival penicillin in cost but old-style medicinal compounds in effectiveness. Just as the advice to 'take two aspirin and go to bed' holds its own against fancier and more expensive remedies for physical ailments, the advice 'to take two hours and read a book' is not easily surpassed as a remedy for obsolescence.

One of our problems in seeking better cures is to know whom to treat. Although the ravages of obsolescence are most easily measured in the decay of institutions like business firms, schools, armies, government agencies, hospitals or churches, the vaccine or medicine must fundamentally be chosen to act on the individuals who lead such institutions. Both Wilensky (1967) in his analysis of 'organizational intelligence' processes, and Drucker (1969), in his prescriptions for 'the age of the knowledge worker,' stress this focus on remaking institutional leadership. They both emphasize that discovering how to manage knowledge workers and how to stimulate and guide search and learning processes throughout an organization is the key management challenge for the coming decades. Bennis (1966) Levinson (1968) and others build on similar themes as they point out the need for managers to become better initiators and orchestraters of change.

Managers must become better under difficult and conflicting conditions. For organizations to prosper in a human and political sense, managers are being pressed to give the diverse individuals they manage a larger voice in goal setting and decision making. At the same time, the increasing size and technological complexity of organizations create counter-pressures toward centralization, tight coordination and subordination of the individual, in the interest of efficiency in achieving goals. Although in seeking ways to improve and to balance these pressures, issues of organizational design are involved, no recommendations for organizing will substitute for the leader who fights obsolescence for himself and who works to help his fellow managers and professionals fight, too.

Yet the more one watches the supposed victims of obsolescence, the more one must ask who wants the cure. Against inevitabilities of the human life cycle, against pressures of organizational life, and against difficulties inherent in any serious effort to learn, it may in face seem comfortable, even natural, satisfying, and rational to let one's competence and skills decay. Personal initiative is directed much more easily toward other targets than preventing obsolescence. Hence, in looking for ways by which we might stimulate people to learn, we should focus first on some of the reasons why for most individuals obsolescence is a tolerable disease.

## SOME FACTS OF LIFE

Any discussion must start with the obvious fact that life is finite. Age as it relates to what physiology, attitudes, and social traditions allow is an index to man's responsiveness to continuing education.

The main problem is not, as is commonly believed, that with passing years people lose physiologically the capacity to learn. At least during the years before normal retirement, most individuals do not in any fundamental sense get too old to learn, not even too old to learn complex intellectual or organizational skills. Some studies show that older people learn more slowly, but in compensation, that what they do learn is better focused and more error free. You can teach old dogs new tricks.

If the capacity to learn new knowledge and skills does decline with age, it probably declines more from lack of practice and lack of encouragement than for physiological reasons. If intellectual prowess is in any way analogous to physical prowess, as research suggests it is, exercising the mind may be as important as exercising the heart. Jogging or calisthenics as physical programs are only effective if done strenuously and regularly over long periods of time. Mental jogging is no less strict a regimen and offers no easy short-cuts. The occasional one-day seminar does no more for a soft head than weekend golf does for a soft stomach. The longer such an easy course is pursued, the harder it is to regain lost ground.

Sustained practice in learning falls victim to many basic life pressures, some of which have little directly to do with a man's job or organizational affiliations. Among many commentators on attitudes toward learning in relation to age, Henry (1961) observes in his studies of managers that the 30's tend to be years of self-confidence, activity, and focus on getting ahead. The 40's are years in which doubts on personal identity and questions about life patterns and life objectives—last raised in adolsecence—reappear. The 50's are often years of declining interest in 'action,' less intense participation, and retreat. Back and Gergen (1963) note that older persons in public opinion polls are more likely than younger ones to have a limited time and space perspective and to favor drastic solutions to complex social problems. Taguiri found that executives arriving at senior management programs had fewer self-perceived development needs than executives arriving at middle management programs.

Such trends can be understood, as Melville Dalton's classic study of *Men Who Manage* (1959) shows, in terms of the flow of forces and pressures a man feels in his organizational life; but some of these trends may have less to do with the job situation than we commonly assume.

Taguiri has tried to relate attitudes toward learning and perceived development needs to the family concerns that middle and senior executives face. They are faced with the challenges of understanding and working with their adolescent children, and the questions their children raise may prompt the basic doubts and self-examination that they begin to experience. There are additional burdens of financial and familial support, both for children away in college and for aging parents and relatives.

Taguiri ties his analysis back to the thinking of men like Erik Erikson (1959). In Erikson's view, during the years spanned by a normal working career, a man confronts three major life dilemmas. The first, in the 20's, involves making choices among the alternatives that have been explored during adolescence, but basically choices between closeness and distance, between cooperativeness and comptetitiveness or aloofness in work and social relationships.

In mid-career, at the time Henry talks about self-doubt and questioning, Erikson highlights the choice between 'generativity' and 'self-absorption.' Some persons, capitalizing on things that life has opened for them, become even more energetically engaged. For them, presumably, obsolescence is not likely to be a problem. For others there is energetic engagement, but a shift in emphasis from self to children or to younger associates or students, as the case may be. For such persons, we may not be concerned with obsolescence unless it somehow warps the counsel they give to those they are trying to help. But for a third category of person, these middle years are times of overbearing problems and stresses, of a kind that absorb energy and attention in ways that make it hard for those involved to even recognize such 'small matters' as the threat of professional obsolescence.

In the final years of a career or the early years of retirement, Erikson sees the pressures growing again toward a crisis between man's search for meaning and integrity in life as he is living it and feelings of despair and disgust when he contemplates his own decline and death. The first obviously can be a profound stimulus for learning and renewal, even late in life; the second implies feelings that renewal is a hopeless cause.

In a world where it is hard to untangle what is physical, what is psychological, and what is cultural, it is still relatively easy to appreciate the joint result. Much as we talk about the need to counter obsolescence as persons age in our society, aging persons themselves are not expected to learn as much, to work as hard, or to be as concerned about renewal. Such expectations seem deeply ingrained; and because they are, they affect the kinds of jobs, training opportunities, and counseling that we offer. Expectations plus tangible actions and decisions based on these expectations, in turn, can reinforce inappropriately and prematurely feelings of indifference or despair among managers and professionals about the value of self-renewal efforts. All these factors combine, quite apart from counter efforts which may be mounted by a particular profession or organization, to make it rational for men, as they age, to assume the inevitability of obsolescence. All these factors erect barriers that typical approaches toward combatting obsolescence are weak in overcoming.

It is not clear what the remedies should be. I would suggest, however, that it does little good to try to solve the problem simply by increasing people's anxiety about not taking enough time to maintain or enhance their skills. It may do a great deal of good to assume, even if it may be an oversimplification, that age is not a barrier to the ability to learn. With the extra measure of confidence which this assumption can give to those we are trying to help, we should then try to become more perceptive about how the timing of renewal opportunities, the incentives that we use for involvement in learning, and the structure and content of what we offer can be varied to suit a man's total life involvements, not just his immediate job situation.

## PERVERSITIES OF PURPOSIVE ORGANIZATIONS

If the natural cycle of life tends to divert men from concern about self-renewal, the organizations for which they work and to which the benefits of renewal might accrue divert and discourage men still further. For all the emphasis in recent years on change as a way of life in organizations, the theories and traditions on which we base most of our practice of management do not assume learning is a major goal. Organizations are far more prone to accept and exploit an individual's independent efforts at renewal and growth than they are to encourage and guide such efforts. Such encouragement as there is is too often sporadic and ambiguous.

Let us consider some of the problems. As a matter of tradition and of real environmental pressures, organizations think and measure in terms of *doing*, not *learning*. If THINK, for example, is the slogan that gave IBM its public image, SELL and INSTALL is the current motto that is burned in the consciousness of its field force—and may well be the one that had most to do with establishing IBM's record of growth. If immediate short-term results are not good, no organization has a chance to concern itself about the long-run.

Even in our growing concern for planning as a major organizational activity, the literature so far has little to say about the processes of individual growth and renewal that can keep a planning function fresh. The books and articles focus on how individuals can do a better job, alone and collectively, of sizing up opportunities and problems and getting feedback on the results of actions—*within the range of the knowledge and skills that each planner currently possesses.* But none of the major works on planning yet ties the design of a planning system back to the related design problem of setting up effective programs for developing the managers and professionals responsible for putting plans together and carrying them out.

Until we can do a better job of planning within and across organizations, we stand in danger of what Dr. York in his paper has documented: failure to foresee even foreseeable shifts in manpower needs and distortion of educational priorities and job recruitment incentives to the point that even newly trained professionals cannot find jobs in the areas for which they trained. The vicitims of poor planning are generally not the planners, but the technicians and middle managers who sometimes seem to have 'low motivations' to combat obsolescence. What seems to be low motivation may in fact derive from a feeling that they have little control over the direction or level of technology that governs their futures or over policies that lead to their replacement by younger, differently or more recently trained men. The current state of the art in professional manpower planning may be doing a great deal more to promote unionization than it is doing to promote regeneration.

Why is the emphasis on *doing* detrimental to fighting obsolescence, and why is the growing interest in planning not enough? First, *doing* implies a short-range perspective. As a manager or professional engages in short-range tasks and is measured by short-range results, he is readily forced into habits of allocating his time and energies that run counter to his mounting any sustained effort at developing new knowledge and skills. It is the problems of time management on the job, in fact, that have led many industrial training specialists to the conclusion that learning can only take place at times and in places where the learner is totally disengaged from ongoing job pressures. Too easily, perhaps, we have won the battle to get a man's attention for learning by taking him away from his job, only to lose the battle of showing him how what we teach can be used when he returns to his normal working environment.

Second, the results of *doing,* as perceived by the doer, do little to highlight needs to learn. As he sees the results of actions, whether cognitively as feedback or emotionally as positive or negative reinforcement, only the proximate causes of the results are likely to be visible. A man may see that he overlooked a key variable when he proposed his solution or made his decision. The same man, however, is much less likely to understand that he could have prevented that and other oversights by a concerted effort, two years before, to upgrade his understanding of politics, engineering, economics, or the competitive environment. The cost of missing a significant opportunity to learn seldom becomes apparent until it seems too late to recoup.

Even observations based on the cumulative results of short-term actions and decisions can be misleading. If promotion opportunities in an organization truly depended on the extent to which a man developed his knowledge and skills and if there were real penalties in status or salary for failing to undertake the fight against obsolescence, our problem would be much simpler than it is. In fact, however, we live in a world where a jest like the Peter Principle (Peter & Hull 1969), that every man rises until he reaches his level of incompetence, rings true for many readers and a world where serious efforts to model the process of upward movement in an organizational hierarchy show that a model which assumes random choice of candidates for advancement predicts as well as one which tries to take into account the quality of the candidates' actions and decisions.

To make a more accurate and less cynical assumption, even if men who do reach top positions in management and the professions are men who devote unusual amounts of time and effort to conscious and planned expansion of their capabilites, the power of their example is largely lost on the people it should influence. Often they do their reading or carry on their most productive exploratory conversations with people who can teach them new things away from the office and after hours. Thus, those who should profit from their example seldom see how painstakingly they have built their knowledge and experience. Often, too, in offering themselves as models to younger managers and professionals, they confuse the substance of what they have learned with the basic processes and motivations involved. In a changing world, the younger manager or professional needs to imitate a self-renewing superior in level of energy and scope of effort as he tries to build his own understanding. However, the old knowledge and skills that his superior can offer or the sources of information and experience that his superior might recommend may be hopelessly out of date. Particularly for the man at mid-career, the job of seeking appropriate personal models to guide his efforts to learn includes examining younger and more recently trained men below him and persons with contrasting ideas in other organizations as well as looking upward at the men who have gone before. The traditions of hierarchical organizations place too much stress on looking inward and upward, too little on looking downward and out.

Finally, the pace at which many organizations move today leaves little time for careful and considered programs of development and growth for the individual. As Robert White notes, 'The nurturing of growth requires the long patience of the husbandman rather than the hasty intervention of the mechanic.' Yet too often we do not show the patience or foresight of even a good mechanic. How does one make time for growth on a planned basis for the manager or professional who is immersed in his job ten to fourteen hours a day, sometimes six or seven days a week? How does one sustain any kind of long-range plan for his progress in organizations which may change his manager or his place of work every two or three years? How does one build any continuity between on-the-job learning and formal training programs when a large share of formal training, particularly in the most critical and advanced areas of professional or management training is done by itinerant lecturers and seminar leaders who have little pre-class knowledge of the students or their organizations?

Ironically, the diversionary pressures on time and other resources may be greatest in those organizations that are most caught up in the problems of change. Anyone who has talked recently with a university president, the mayor of a large city, or the head of a technology-based corporation knows that for him and his staff the demands of contending with the immediate challenges and crises of their environment tax them to the limit. They have much greater appreciation than leaders of most other kinds of institutions for the costs of obsolescence and often have much better ideas of how, in the abstract, to attack the problem. On the other hand, unfortunately, they sometimes have less time and energy left over to give to the effort.

For both subconscious and conscious reasons, then, organizations like individuals may be more aware of the general issue of obsolescence than they are prepared to act against it. There may be some benefits to be derived from the threat of an apocalyptic end to life on this planet, from the thought that total collapse of society is possible in *our* generation rather than only for some remote future generation. However, increasing anxieties about organizational survival probably has little more therapeutic value than increasing anxieties for the individual. Neither is tinkering with organization charts or procedures likely to help much.

One of the things that does matter is that there be a convincing example from those whose behavior and advice command attention, that continuing self-education is important. It must be seen as important at the expense of other things that now command priority on the job, since for almost anyone whose obsolescence would be really detrimental, it is unreasonable to demand more time at the expense of family and other interests. To guide and direct efforts at self-renewal, the other thing which matters is research on feedback and reward systems which will force men and their managers to seek and analyze underlying, long-term causes for successes and failures in performance, as well as the proximate causes which now receive most attention.

## THE DISCOMFORTS OF LEARNING

In addition to facing and life-cycle organizational pressures that make the fight against obsolescence seem like a low priority diversionary activity, men find that the fight is lonely, difficult and often unrewarding.

We suggested earlier an analogy between keeping fit physically and staying alive intellectually. Learning is not accomplished by occasional access to information or experience, any more than physical conditioning is accomplished by watching a football game. Learning means active effort on a sustained basis to seek and absorb information, to coalesce experience into knowledge and skills, and to apply and evaluate results. Education comes not by exposure to, but by engagement with the world.

How far, for example, do our thoughts about combatting obsolescence go beyond an effort to increase a man's access to information? To the extent that information access or retrieval is our major focus, we are ignoring the possibility that most men may already have access to more, quantitatively, than they need. In fact, reconstruction of events like the bombing of Pearl Harbor, the decision of the Chinese to intervene in Korea, or the introduction of the Edsel suggest that it is very easy to get trapped in elaborate networks of gathering and processing information, often better inter-pretation of less complete and less sophisticated information can lead to greater understanding and better decisions.

I have been working in the field of data processing for the past five years, and it is a rare month when at least one new journal or information service relating to data processing does not cross my desk. The marginal value of a new source of information is almost nothing, however, compared to the marginal value to an insight or an experience or a question that forces me to think more deeply about the things I am already reading. One of the great defects of the free market for publications and information services in the United States, at least, is that the entrepreneurs have been much more effective in expanding the flow of information and unnecessary duplica-tion of coverage than they have been in offering 'handles' to improve the qualitative search, evaluation, and assimilation of information.

How far have we gone in improving a man's skill in asking questions, both to discover and to evaluate information? Some of the best guides to self-education might be developed around the theme of how to ask good questions. In this, fields like clinical medicine or forensic law are far ahead of fields like engineering or management. For management and the related support professions, developments in the field of statistics have probably been most productive. Concepts of sampling and of hypothesis testing, Bayesian or other, can provide powerful guides to thinking and learning, even in situations far removed from the normal domains of statistical analysis. We have done less well, in helping people understand and correct for bias, intentional and uninten-tional, in sources of information. We deal with information too often as if it were produced and communicated in a benign, cooperative and orderly world. Instead, it is a world that is in fact conflicted, competitive, and often disorderly and confused, a world where there is often greater profit in the retransmission of information than in its reevaluation. The manager who would learn needs the same skills for understanding what goes wrong in the formulation and transmission of human communications that a skilled trial lawyer needs for cross-examination, that a psychiatrist needs to get to the root of his patient's troubles, or that a consultant needs to validate his client's statement of a problem. He needs the skills of an adversary, the ability to resolve suspicion or evidence of bias by asking questions.

The skill of question-asking is even more important, given the tendency of most men to prefer to learn via verbal rather than written contact with information sources. Studies show that even communications among engineers and scientists, for whom the discipline of documented transmission of new knowledge is best developed, there is a preference for oral questioning and personal contact over systematic search of the literature.

These same studies also confirm the high value that is placed by many learners simply on the opportunity to browse rather than on more complex facilities for systematic search. They also reinforce the idea of Drucker and Wilensky that in the absence of strong values for browsing and interpersonal communication, organizational changes that reduce barriers to communication have little effect.

## PERSONAL INITIATIVE AS A DAILY CONCERN

How de we stimulate a greater degree of personal initiative in the fight against professional and managerial obsolescence? We can only develop initiative on a day-by-day basis. Our strategy must become one of preventing, not curing the problem.

The answer does not lie in dramatizing the costs of letting one's skills and abilities decay. A whole range of studies, focused on everything from the prevention of murder to the prevention of tooth decay, suggest that warnings of dire long-range consequences have little effect. It is more important to provide as positive models leaders and senior professionals who demonstrate in visible ways that taking time to explore, to question, to learn, and to make mistakes as one learns are approved priority behaviours. Those who follow the models or who strike out on their own need feedback and reinforcement that acknowledges and rewards the act of trying to learn as much as it does the results.

An effort to reward and encourage initiative toward learning in small stages is important. By the time a man realizes that his knowledge and skills are out of date, and especially by the time he sees the implications of such neglect for himself and his organization, the task of catching up seems impossible. Too often there is no will and no confidence about fighting back.

'Reward' can mean some simple things. Properly it means praising and commending, but it often means simply noticing and talking about a man's efforts to build new areas of competence. In situations where the effort to learn comes at the expense of short-term mistakes, reward may only mean not mentioning the mistake. It can, more often than we realize, mean the thoughtfulness of considered and detailed criticism which focuses on helping a man decide how to expand his skills. Despite our fondness today for elaborate appraisal systems, timidity about engaging in appraisals is widespread. Regular exchanges, upward and downward, of evaluations between man and manager can go a long way toward stimulating learning efforts as a natural part of the job.

Managers must be prepared to note, to encourage and to reward unorthodox kinds of initiative. Encouraging learning, as we have known since the times of Eve's apple and Pandora's box, can distrub and disrupt an organization. If we are not willing to run the risk, we are hypocritical to concern ourselves about obsolescence.

As Drucker reminds us in *The Age of Discontinuity* (1969), managers of knowledge workers should expect that serious efforts to refresh old skills or to develop new ones are likely to lead to discontent, to questions, and to defections from an organization. We must recognize and respect the fact that some of our best arguments for continuing growth and development among employees relate to their personal self-interest, not to the interests of the organization. Personal initiative, if directed partly toward opening up new career opportunities or greater satisfactions off the job, is much more likely to take hold and feed on itself.

Although defections give ulcers to personnel managers, they can be healthy for the organization and for the man who moves. Increased evidence that drastic changes in career pattern can work out successfully boost the numbers of people who will engage in substantial self-education to qualify for such changes. Increased flows of people between organizations at mid-career provides a freshening of opportunities and perspectives in both the sending and receiving organization.

Organizations which reward learning and the translation of learning into action will have to be more loosely coupled than many organizations are today. Old style manuals of organization stress hierarchial and workflow relationships that are logical and orderly. The new style manual must put more emphasis on juxtaposition and confrontation of individuals and groups for educational, as well as performance reasons. The chief stimulus for learning even for scientists and engineers, is human interaction. The chief danger of old-style ways of organizing is that human interactions get routinized and stale. People can afford to work a little harder, walk a little further, take a little longer to accomplish things with associates on whom they routinely depend for cooperative efforts in their daily jobs. They should find it easier, closer, faster, however, to be in converstaion with someone who is likely to suggest a new idea, ask a new question, or force an off-beat effort at problem solving.

A good organization, like a good boullabaisse, always involves some surprises in the way things are mixed together.

## NEW TECHNOLOGIES FOR SELF-EDUCATION

Parallel to efforts to improve day-to-day motivations for learning, greater ingenuity is needed to make resources available. Most of our effort is still going into marginal enhancements of books and lectures. Text publishers prosper, even when a writer like Marshal McLuhan uses text himself to proclaim the declining influence of the printed word. The ranks of American circuit riders in executive development include at least one spell-binder who lectures about self-discipline and self-development for three—four hours without stopping or taking questions.

Genuinely low-cost audiotape cartridge players and potentially low-cost videotape cartridge units are beginning to make audiovisual presentations as easy to distribute widely, as easy to use on flexible and individualized study schedules as printed matter. Small audiotape players share with books the advantage of portability, though videotape players are still cumbersome and fragile to move around.

Audiovisual media can be used creatively to let many students share the ideas of a single skilled teacher or to help demonstrate and explain graphically complex, dynamic phenomena. Effective use for instruction, however, requires a degree of professionalism and expense in preparation of materials that most organizations will not commit. Hence, there is a largely unfilled gap between well designed but general and elementary tapes and films for mass audiences and locally produced materials, tailored for local needs but of home movie quality.

Educational technology must move beyond its focus on modes of presentation. The real gains will come as we begin to design aids that prompt thinking about the definition of new problems, inquiry about possible solutions, and experimentation and evaluation of possible approaches. Here, the promise of the computer as a supplement to other media looks brightest.

We are beginning to have, with lower cost machines and widespread availability of systems and terminals, a way of providing access to computers on a large scale to managers and professionals who wish to learn. We have a good deal of experience now in the design of languages and modeling techniques that let us simulate on the computer parts of the world we would like people to learn about. After a period of mistaken assignment of roles, when we expected the computer to present information and ask questions of the students, we are now revising our ideas about computer-assisted instruction to put more emphasis on having the computer represent possible states of a system or of 'the world' and letting the student learn by asking questions of the computer.

We have a long way to go. Most efforts to devise inquiry-based learning systems on the computer or to achieve widespread use of simulation or simulation games have fallen short because of cost and because of inadequate theories for designing the man-machine interaction to achieve particular learning objectives. This is, however, a direction of promise. It is a direction, from direct evidence with CAI and with simulation games, that makes students excited about learning. It provides, to the extent that the simulation allows, a way of learning lessons in an artificial environment that would be costly and painful to learn in real life.

With computers as with human contracts, the main message we must keep in mind is that the kind of learning we care about—the kind that is involved in rebuilding the skills and competence of managers and professionals at mid-career—must be an active, an engaging, an exciting, and a rewarding process. We have touched on some of the reasons why initiative to forestall obsolescence does not appear, and on a few approaches that might be used to encourage its appearance. We have called for understanding and ingenuity on the part of those who want to solve the problem. We would also counsel patience. To quote Robert White (1952):

> The nurturing of growth . . . requires waiting for impulse to declare itself, for interest to appear, for intiative to come forth. It calls for a tolerant attitude toward individuality, respect for the unique pattern that unfolds in every case. It demands confidence that in the long run individuality will be an asset, not a handicap, and that it will lead both to a happier life and to a better world than if the goal had been set at conformity, pleasantness, marketability, or a pattern that is merely the empty logical opposite of mental and emotional disorder.

## REFERENCES

Back, K. W. & Gergen, K. J. Individual orientations, public opinion, and the study of internation relations. *Social Problems,* Summer 1963, *11*, 77–87.

Bennis, W. *Changing organizations.* New York: McGraw-Hill, 1966.

Dalton, M. *Men who manage.* New York: John Wiley, 1959.

Drucker, P. F. *The age of discontinuity.* New York: Harper & Row, 1969.

Erikson, E. Identity and the life cycle. *Psychological Issues,* 1959, *1* (1).

Henry, W. Conflict, age and the executive. *Business Topics,* Spring 1961, 15–25.

Levinson, H. *The exceptional executive.* Cambridge, Mass.: Harvard University Press, 1968.

Peter, L. J. & Hull, R. *The Peter principle.* New York: Morrow, 1969.

White, R. *Lives in progress.* New York: Dryden, 1952.

Wilenski, H. L. *Organizational intelligence.* New York: Basic Books, 1967.

# Combatting Obsolescence Using Perceived Discrepancies in Job Expectations of Research Managers and Scientists

Gerald V. Barrett
Bernard M. Bass
John A. Miller

Management Research Center,
University of Rochester.

## INTRODUCTION

### The Problem of Obsolescence

The future world of work has been the subject of considerable prognostication by scholars and businessmen, particularly recently. While these predictions differ widely, they do augur a world vastly different from the present one. Today's professional, therefore, is faced with the very real danger of becoming obsolete—today's skills and knowledge will not enable him to operate effectively in tomorrow's professional world.

Serious predictions and forebodings have appeared in the literature of many disciplines, outlining, likely directions of change in the future. Most professionals have probably read numerous forecasts on future directions likely in their own fields. But how many have actually reflected on what this means to them and their future careers? How many have taken steps toward identifying those areas in which training or retraining is essential to progress in their careers?

Professionals today often spend upward of 60 hours per week at their jobs, and may argue that with this kind of daily pressure, it is difficult, if not impossible, to find the time for introspection. As it is, they may argue, they can not find enough time to think clearly about their own day-to-day problems, so how can they be expected to find the time to think about their long-term goals? Furthermore, if the organization decides that its professionals require certain kinds of training, the organization will make sure they receive that training. But to rely on these arguments is to court obsolescence. A professional must take on himself the responsibility for keeping up with progress in his chosen field; only he can prevent his own obsolescence. He must plan for his own continuing development, and take responsibility for following up on his plan (Haas, 1969).

### The Need for Self-Development

The transition from predictions of the future to the formulation of a plan for self-development is often a difficult one to make, and may in part account for most professionals' lack of such plans. One of the purposes of the program of research presently underway at the Management Research Center is to develop techniques which make the bridging of this gap between predictions and action plans possible—to enable professionals to describe where they are, where they want to go, and when and how to get there. And it is they who must participate in the decision process. They can not remain in the stance of the proverbial reluctant student challenging his instructor with: 'I dare you teach me something!'

**Organizational involvement.**

For Schein (1964) the process involves the organization as well, requiring an interest on its part to . . .

> . . . influence the beliefs, attitudes and values . . . of an individual for the purpose of "developing" him, i.e. changing him in a direction which the organization regards to be *in his own* and the organization's best interests (p. 331, emphasis ours).

But it is a two-way affair. For the aims of a development program to be realized, its contents must be understood and accepted by members of the organization (Drucker, 1953), and this requires concern for individual needs. Thus, Chowdhry (1963) found a greater involvement in the development process if the idea of attending is self-initiated and if the participants are involved in decisions regarding their own training and development. Also there must be some assurance that results of the training will be of use to the man himself (i.e., that positive transfer of learning will occur), that he is equipped with the basic skill or knowledge upon which the training activities will be built, and that an adequate opportunity will be provided for learning to occur (Bellows, Gilson, & Odiorne, 1962, Chapter 3).

In depicting a 'persuasion' model of change, Schein (1964) perceives development as a 'process of influence' involving *unfreezing* of old patterns of behavior: *changing* into new ones; and *refreezing,* or internalizing these new patterns [1].

*Approaches.* Development is accomplished using a variety of methods, some quite recent. Since the computer has come into use, new techniques of training, such as simulation and 'business games' have appeared. The development effort has been updated in other ways as well. For example, many organizations have separate programs for different age groups to account for elapsed time and different content of prior formal educational backgrounds (Dunn, 1967). Bernthal (1963) has described a continuum of management training, ranging from the intellectual methods (lectures, guided discussions and conferences); to vicarious experiences (case study, incident method, role play and simulation); to social awareness (T-groups); and finally complete behavioral transformation (psychotherapy and psychoanalysis). This learning may be acquisitional, experiential or exploratory (Dill, Crowston and Elton, 1965), and may include: 1) technical knowledge and information relative to their own job; 2) broader understanding of functions other than their own; 3) skills in decision making and human relations; 4) motivation to acquire and apply the preceding three (Bursk, 1967).

*The importance of the individual.* The role of the individual in professional

---

[1] Levinson (1962) addresses himself to the importance of identification in the change process. He points out that where a development staff does the actual training, the opportunity for identification is not provided. He suggests that trainees be taught principles of coaching and counseling in order that they may, in turn, be the developers, thus permitting identification to take place. Leigh (1966) espouses a similar view. Levinson also points out why coaching often fails today.

development is crucial. It is not enough simply to have training programs available to professionals or to submit them to various kinds of development programs. They must *want* to undergo training. But many professionals tend to be motivated more by today's challenges than by tomorrow's; more by current than future performance. In his own self-interest, however, a professional cannot afford to let today's pressures preclude his thinking about tomorrow's world of work and his role in it. Thus a large part of a successful development effort is to increase the professional's own desire to learn. 'A man who *wants* to develop himself does—a man who wants to *be developed* rarely is (Hull, 1964, p. 39).' 'Ideally, . . . each . . . should go through a careful process of self-examination, and if necessary, indoctrination (Berkwit, 1966, p. 107).' The ultimate goal of the organization should be, as Gardner (1963) suggests, 'to shift to the individual the burden of pursuing his own education (p. 12).'

### Requirements for Self-Education

Self-education involves at least three steps: 1) establishing a learning agenda; 2) planning a strategy for learning; and 3) evaluating the chances for success (Dill, Crowston & Elton, 1965). Although particularly important, Dill Crowston & Elton (1965) note that 'well-stated learning agendas proved to be rare among our inter-viewees (p. 121).'

Included in the learning agenda are:
1. Statements of *aims*—changes that they would like to make in their knowledge, skills, attitudes, values, or relationships with other men and organizations.

2. Definitions of *areas for study, search, reflection,* or *testing*—lists of activities, experiences, or questions that can help them accomplish their aims.

3. Ideas about *priorities*—feelings of preference or urgency about what should be learned first (p. 120, numbers provided).

As will be seen the procedures for individual participants in our development research program fit squarely with the Dill *et al* proposal. Each individual (1) develops his own learning agenda; (2) plans some tactics at least, if not strategies to begin working on the agenda; and (3) evaluates the chances of success with the help of knowledgeable colleagues.

### THE DEVELOPMENT RESEARCH PROGRAM

#### Objectives of the Program

Within this conceptual framework, the Professional Development Research Program at the Management Research Center has undertaken a number of studies of self-development methods in professional populations. A first set of studies in this area investigated the expectations and plans of managers in several U.S. manufacturing firms (Haas, 1969).

A second concentrates on providing undergraduate college students with materials to assist them in self-development activities (Bass, Krusell, & Vicino, 1970).

The prime purpose of the third set of studies in the program is to evaluate experimentally the relative effectiveness of a number of self-development techniques designed to motivate Research & Development personnel to undertake specific actions in preparation for their future careers.

The basic concerns behind these experimental studies are the urgently recognized needs for methods to be employed in R & D organizations to combat technological obsolescence of R & D personnel and also to help assure the development of managerial competence in R & D organizations.

As by-products of the research, benefits are envisaged both to the individuals who participate, in the form of personal planning and education, and to the organizations involved, in the form of a survey of the preferences (attitudes) and expectations of R & D personnel about changes they foresee taking place in a wide variety of areas related to their work. This survey also enables identification of those areas which R & D personnel see as of key importance over the next five years, as well as those factors seen as being under the control of the individual.

**Research Method**

The instruments for data collection include a Questionaire (Q) concerning the individual's preferences and expectations about a wide range of conditions in his future world of work. They also include an opportunity for the participant to state specific steps he wants to take, in the form of Action Plans (AP), and an opportunity to clarify his plans and commit himself to action through discussion and feedback (D) sessions.

Each of these elements (Q, AP, and D) is likely to generate some results in terms of thinking, action, or commitment to action on the part of the participant. All three elements (Q + AP + D) have been incorporated into Exercise Future (Miller, Haas, Bass, & Ryterband, 1970), one of a program of exercises for individual and group development initiated by the Management Research Center and used in a wide variety of organizational settings (Bass, 1970).

In summary, the research is designed to permit evaluation of the relative effectiveness of these elements of the individual's planning process in motivating to undertake specific steps in preparing for his future career.

**PURPOSE**

The present paper reports preliminary findings of the first phase of the Research and Development study described above. These findings focus only on responses to the questionnaire portion (Q) of Exercise Future, which deal with the preferences and expectations of R & D personnel about their future world of work.

The purpose of this report is to note certain aspects of these preferences and expectations which bear on the requirements for training and development efforts in R & D organizations. Several elements of these findings imply the need for organization-based efforts; they may also be useful as a guide to individuals in planning and carrying out self-development activities.

# METHOD

## Subjects

The subjects in this investigation were 143 male research and development personnel from a major U.S. Government laboratory who volunteered for the study. The sample consisted of scientists, engineers, and technical managers; all had civilian status. The mean age was 39, with approximately 70 per cent between the ages of 30 and 50. Approximately 60 per cent of the group had worked in the organization six or more years.

## Research Instrument

Exercise Future (Miller, Haas, Bass, & Ryterband, 1970) was administered to all the experimental subjects. The exercise was designed to allow participants to explore specific expectations of their future world of work and to help them determine the implications this would have in preparing for the future.

A total of 46 questions, grouped into eight areas, are responded to by each subject. First, each respondent individually indicates his preference for each of the 46 items on a one to five rating scale going from 'I ideally would *prefer* [this condition] to *decrease* greatly in the next five years' to 'I ideally would *prefer* [it] to *increase* greatly in the next five years.' Next, the respondent indicates his *expectation* about what is likely to happen on each item using a similar five-point scale. Next the respondent notes the importance to him of each item, indicating it to be of great or little importance. Last he registers the amount of control (much or little), he perceives to have over each item. (See Figure 1, which illustrates a portion of the questionnaire.)

Thus, the respondent provides data concerning his attitudes (preferences) about job requirements. Given his preference on an item, a comparison with his realistic expectation permits an analysis of a possible discrepancy. This may, in turn, signal the need for action to be taken to prepare for a future world of work which is seen to be at variance with preferences. If the respondent believes the item to be of importance to him and also subject to his control, he may be motivated to undertake efforts aimed at increasing necessary skills or changing job requirements. If, on the other hand, he feels no ability to control the area, he may be led to a re-examination of his attitude concerning it. At the extreme, a large number of discrepancies between preferences and expectations in areas of importance seen as outside the respondent's control may trigger sufficient dissatisfaction to predict withdrawal from the organization.

The items are grouped under the following headings: educational upgrading, reward structure, organizational requirements, interpersonal-intergroup relations, external concerns, computer effects, and organizational objectives. These clusters were developed from factor analyses of the responses of engineers and managers to a longer questionnaire (Haas, 1969). Organizational objectives and external concerns will not be discussed in this report since the items in those categories were less germane to our sample of respondents.

## FIGURE 1
## EXCERPTS FROM FUTURE WORLD OF WORK QUESTIONNAIRE,
## PART OF EXERCISE FUTURE

| | A | B | C | D | E |
|---|---|---|---|---|---|
| **SAMPLE ITEMS** | PREFER (Ideally would like) | EXPECT | DIFFERENCE (Col. A–Col. B) | IMPORTANT TO ME | CONTROL |
| | 5 = great increase 1 = great decrease | | | x = much o = little | |

EDUCATIONAL UPGRADING

1. Importance of my knowing analytical techniques of decision-making

2. Need for additional knowledge in my field of specialization

3. My skill in attending to many and diverse kinds of information

4. Time spent by me in my own development and training

5. Importance of reading fast and effectively

6. Importance of writing effectively

7. Importance of speaking effectively

For *COLUMN A:*

I IDEALLY WOULD PREFER
the condition to:

For *COLUMN B:*

I ACTUALLY EXPECT
the condition to:

5 – *Increase greatly* over the next five years
4 – Increase *to some extent*
3 – Stay the same
2 – Decrease *to some extent*
1 – *Decrease greatly*

For *COLUMN C:*

Subtract COLUMN B from COLUMN A, without regard to sign. Many of these entries will be 0; the maximum difference is, of course, 5-1 or 1-5 = 4.

For *COLUMN D:*

The IMPORTANCE of this
condition to me, or the amount
of effect this has on me is:

For *COLUMN E:*

The amount of CONTROL or
influence I have over this
condition is:

X – Very much
O – Comparatively little

(From Miller, et al., 1970, pp. 2, 3)

TABLE 1

SURVEY OF SELECTED RESPONSES TO EXERCISE FUTURE

| *Educational Upgrading* | *Preferred Increase* | *Expected Increase* | *Impor-tant* | *Much Control* |
|---|---|---|---|---|
| 1. Skill in attending to many and diverse kinds of information | 88* | 83 | 82 | 62 |
| 2. Time spent by me in my own development and training | 73 | 44 | 91 | 76 |
| 3. Need for additional knowledge in my field or specialization | 82 | 80 | 87 | 64 |
| *Reward Structure* | | | | |
| 1. Importance of my having up-to-date technical knowledge in determining salary increases | 63 | 38 | 72 | 34 |
| 2. Importance of my professional reputation (with clients, financial sources, professional colleagues) in determining my rewards | 64 | 48 | 76 | 50 |
| 3. Importance of my knowledge of management principles and practices in determining my promotions or salary increases | 67 | 58 | 66 | 36 |
| *Organizational Structure* | | | | |
| 1. Freedom to follow my own interests in selecting new projects or activities | 70 | 28 | 89 | 34 |
| 2. Freedom to set my own daily work schedule | 48 | 23 | 76 | 44 |
| 3. The number of activities (Projects, groups, products, etc.) I am involved in or responsible for at any one time | 50 | 54 | 65 | 45 |
| *Interpersonal-Intergroup Relations* | | | | |
| 1. Shift from making decisions by myself to group or committee decision-making | 29 | 33 | 61 | 35 |
| 2. Time I spend working alone | 26 | 15 | 56 | 39 |
| 3. Degree to which interpersonal skills ("good human relations") are required for my job | 64 | 61 | 80 | 62 |
| *Computer Effects* | | | | |
| 1. My organization's dependence on computer-generated.information | 55 | 61 | 57 | 30 |
| 2. Importance of knowledge and skill in my organization and computer programming | 59 | 57 | 62 | 36 |
| 3. The power or influence exerted on my organization by managers of computer operations | 12 | 24 | 52 | 19 |

(*all figures expressed in percentages)

## RESULTS

We will focus on only those areas and items which indicate need for action on the part of organizations or individuals (or both) to promote increased self-development efforts among R & D personnel. We assume that such need for action is shown among those items for which:

1) There was substantial preference for change in the next five years,
2) there was substantial expectation of change, or where
3) wide discrepancies were seen by respondents between preferences and expectations. Comments concerning perceived areas of importance and control will also be noted. The results are summarized in Table 1.

The data summarized in Table 1 represent the pooled responses of all 143 research and development personnel. A separate subanalysis was done for those who could be identified as 'managers' (n = 56) and those identified as 'scientists/technicians' (n = 68). The remaining 19 subjects could not be classified unambiguously, and were therefore not included in the subanalysis.

In most areas, no significant differences were found in the responses of these subgroups, relative to each other or to the pooled data. Where such differences were found, they will be noted specifically; otherwise, all comments refer to the pooled results.

### Educational Upgrading

The 143 R & D personnel were clearly aware of their needs for educational upgrading. Respondents expressed these needs in terms of specific expectations in a wide variety of areas. A large majority—between 70 and 85%—expected demands on their reading, writing and speaking skills to increase greatly in the next five years. Moreover, over 80% of the respondents expressed their realization, in terms of both preferences and expectations, that they will require increased knowledge in their own fields of specialization.

Given these specific information and skill areas, the great majority—roughly three-quarters—expressed the desire to spend more time on training and development activities, *but fewer than one-half of the respondents—44%—actually expected to have sufficient time for self-development.* (The subsample of scientists/technicians appeared to be somewhat more intensely concerned about their self-development time than the managerial group.)

It is evident that if personnel believe there are important areas which determine their future over which they have no control, this will play an important part in their self-development. The whole idea of 'fate' orientation has been shown in other contexts to influence behavior. When any cultural group believes that there are many elements in its life which are important but over which it has little control, there is a tendency to forego future planning. In our survey, there are several areas in which respondents express the feeling that they lack control of aspects of their world of work which they consider of importance. This was especially true in the area of educational upgrading.

An overwhelming number of the respondents—91%—saw the time spent by them in their own development and training as being of great importance to them, but only 76% saw themselves as having control over this aspect of their development.

A very high proportion—82%—also believed that their skill in attending to many and diverse kinds of information was extremely important to them, but only 62% viewed this as being under their control. About one-third of the respondents believed that they do not have much control over their ability to remain up-to-date in their technical knowledge, although this item was most frequently judged as being important.

It appears that R & D personnel were generally well aware of the obsolescence problem, but saw relatively little hope of being able to meet their development needs because of the time pressures of short-term activities.

## Reward Structure

Perceptions of the bases of rewards (in terms if promotions, salary increases, and professional reputation) are important determinants of self-development efforts. If organization members do not perceive a link between their development activities and the organization's reward system, the probability of active efforts to update knowledge and skills is lessened.

Thus, for example, although over 80% of the respondents preferred their organizations to stress the importance of having up-to-date knowledge in their respective fields, only 63% saw such knowledge as playing an important role in the determination of salary increases. Further, although 30% saw the possibility of a moderate increase in the degree to which rewards are tied to merit, not one respondent felt that a great increase in the use of merit in determining rewards was likely. (This is probably a realistic expectation; respondents were employed in a government laboratory, under a civil service grading system in which only some of the determinants of salary and promotion are based on merit). Only about one-third expected up-to-date technical knowledge to have an increased impact on promotions and salary increases in the future. About 45% showed a significant gap between their preferences for merit-based rewards and their actual expectations that this link will exist.

As expected, the managerial subsample laid greater stress on knowledge of managerial principles in determining rewards than did the scientists/technicians. Surprisingly, however, a substantial majority of the scientist group agreed with the managers on the importance of knowledge in this area. Seventy-five per cent of the managers would prefer increased emphasis in this area, but so would 62% of the scientists. Seventy-seven per cent of the managers consider knowledge of management principles to be important; 57% of the scientists agree on this.

A key difference between the subgroups was evident in responses concerning control. Most importantly, in neither group did the majority feel they could control the factors influencing rewards, despite their agreement on the importance of these factors. Nevertheless, managers felt more 'in control' (43%) than did the scientists (28%).

Clearly, the Civil Service reward system in this government laboratory provides its members—especially its scientists/technicians—with evidence in support of their expectations that an individual's control of elements which determine his rewards is limited.

These data suggest one reason for the expectation that respondents will not find sufficient time to devote to self-development activities: the expectation was simply that such activities will not be amply rewarded. Thus, at least one organizational implication seems clear: Combatting obsolescence requires that individuals perceive their organizations as rewarding self-development efforts.

## Computer Effects

In general, the R & D personnel were positive toward the computer and its effects upon the organization. They would like to see more importance placed upon programming skill and the use of computer information in their organization. Indeed, over half the respondents preferred that the computer have increased importance; very few want the computer to play a lessened role in the organization.

## Interpersonal-Intergroup Relations

In other areas, the frequency distributions of responses (both for preferences and expectations) tended to be unimodal; there was apparent general agreement on the direction of both preferred and expected change across all subjects in the R & D environment. In the interpersonal-intergroup relations area, however, distributions were clearly bi-modal on several items.

Data collected in another phase of the research program will permit us to associate responses to this questionnaire with other biographical variables, including career goals (e.g., 'technical' *versus* 'managerial'). Our preliminary subanalysis, breaking out manager and scientist/technician subgroups, sheds some light on the differences in preferences discovered in this area. The data suggested splits in preferences based on intentions to focus on either primarily technical career paths, on the one hand, or on managerial paths on the other. Furthermore, there was some indication that the differences seen her may partially be accounted for by age differences and other related variables. For example, 26% of the respondents clearly preferred to have more time to work alone, while 20% wanted less time alone. Similarly, about one-third both preferred and expected greater emphasis on group decision-making activity, but about 20% would prefer far less group activity. For example, 57% of the manager subgroup see time spent in meetings as important, but only about one-third of the scientist/ technician group does. Based on preliminary analyses, we suspect that these differences reflect career commitments. In the absence of further analysis, no generalizations about these items are apparent.

On other items in this area, however, there was evidence of agreement across all subjects in the R & D environment. Sixty-five per cent saw interpersonal skills as an increasingly important (and desirable) aspect of their job requirements. A similar proportion advocate that the organization reflect increasing concern for the values and welfare of employees, but on this item there was a substantial discrepancy between preferences and expectations—the respondents appear to be quite pessimistic about their organization's ability to respond to the needs and desires of individual employees.

## Organizational Requirements

The professional's desire for freedom is amply confirmed in our preliminary data. About 70% desire more freedom to follow their own interests in selecting new projects or activities to work on. Less than 15% expressed any desire to have greater direction in the form of rules and regulations, policies, or decisions from superiors, although about 30% actually expected the organization to provide greater control.

The greatest discrepancy between the preferred and expected was in response to the amount of time spent on administrative paper work. Over 60% expected to spend more time on administrative paper work than they prefer, while only 10% have the reverse expectation. (But 71% of the managerial subgroup perceives adminstrative paper work to be important, while only 37% of the scientist/technician group views it as such).

The issue of control over areas of importance was particularly salient for items dealing with freedom from organizational constraints. There was very high agreement—89%—that the freedom to follow their own research interests in selecting new projects or activities was very important to them, but only a third felt that they had much control over this important aspect of their life. Similarly, three-quarters of the respondents felt that freedom to set their own daily work schedule was very important to them, but only 44% felt they had much control over this. Freedom in project selection and freedom to set daily work schedules are of major importance to most R & D personnel, but they are aspects of life where personnel feel they have considerably less control than they would like to have.

The area where there is the greatest discrepancy between importance and control is that of the organizational rules and regulations. While three-quarters of the respondents believed that this area is very important to them, only eleven per cent believed they had any control at all over the organizational policies which determine what they do. Another large discrepancy was the one dealing with the organization's concern for the values and welfare of the employees. Seventy-five per cent saw this as an important area but barely 17% believed they themselves could have any control over this aspect of the organization's life.

## SUMMARY AND CONCLUSIONS

There is general agreement that 1) the skills and knowledge required of future professionals will be different from those considered sufficient today, and 2) the great majority of today's professionals will require continuous training or substantial retraining if they are to survive in the rapidly changing world or work. As it is now, for example, the status of computer technology is often considerably more advanced than the ability of most R & D professionals to use it effectively.

This initial survey highlights several issues of concern to those involved in the development and utilization of professional man-power. First, the individual employee in our R & D establishment is apparently well aware of his needs for continuous development, but he feels that short-term organizational pressures are likely to impede his ability to achieve his longer-term development goals. Furthermore, he appears to feel that—as an individual—he is relatively powerless in the face of these pressures. This generalization seems particularly true of the scientist/technician group, although the managers agree to a great extent.

We are willing to draw at least one tentative implication in this area. There is a need for organizations to express their concern for the problem of technical obsolescence in tangible ways—in ways which expressly allow sufficient relaxation of day-to-day work pressures so as to provide opportunities for individuals to plan and execute their self-development activities. Furthermore, organizations which are concerned about the problem of obsolescence must provide some evidence that individual development efforts will be rewarded.

A second area concerns the issue of freedom, so often the subject of studies of professional personnel. The respondents in this survey amply confirm other findings in stressing their desires for increased freedom in the selection of projects and the setting of routine schedules, as well as the elimination of constraints in the form of administrative paperwork and organizational rules and regulations. While the issue of freedom is perhaps only indirectly related to the problems of obsolescence and development (in the sense that lack of freedom may also hamper self-development efforts), it undoubtedly plays a role as a determinant of general job satisfaction. Again, clear organizational decisions are required to provide the necessary—and traditionally difficult—balance between the needs of the organization and those of its individual members.

## REFERENCES

Argyle, M. & Smith, T. S. *Training managers.* London: The Acton Society, 1962.

Bass, B. M. Combining Management Training and Research. *Training and Development Journal,* 1967, *21*(4), 2–7.

Bass, B. M., Krusell, J. & Vicino, F. A program of small group exercises for undergraduate student self-development. Annual Report I, Esso Educational Foundation Project, Management Research Center, Rochester, N. Y., June, 2, 1970.

Bellows, R., Gilson, T. Q., & Odiorne, G. S. *Executive skills: Their dynamics and development.* Englewood Cliffs, N.J.: Prentice-Hall, 1962.

Berkwit, G. J. Middle management vs. the computer. *Dun's Review,* November, 1966, 40–42 ff.

Bernthal, W. F. Contributions of the behavioral science approach. *Academy of Management, Proceedings of the Annual Meeting, 1962.* Pittsburgh: Academy of Manangement, 1963.

Bursk, E. C. Education and the corporation. *Management of Personnel Quarterly,* 1967, *6*(3), 2–6.

Chowdhry, K. Management development programs: Executive needs. *Industrial Management Review,* 1963, *4*(2), 31–40.

Dill, W. R., Crowston, W. B. S., & Elton, E. J. Strategies for self-education. *Harvard Business Review,* November-December, 1965, 119–130.

Drucker, P. F. The need for executive development—what it takes to be a good executive. *Advanced Management Journal,* 1953, *18*(1), 5–7.

Dunn, T. W. Key questions on training young executives. *Harvard Business School Bulletin,* 1967, *43*(4), 9–12.

Gardner, J. W. *Self-renewal.* New York: Harper & Row, 1963.

Haas, J. A. Middle managers' expectations of the future world of work: Implications for management development. Technical Report #26, University of Rochester Management Research Center, February, 1969.

House, R. J. *Management development.* Ann Arbor: University of Michigan, Graduate School of Business Administration, Bureau of Industrial Relations, 1967.

Hull, J. W. Management's responsibilities for tomorrow's managers. In Ramo S., Gross, M. W., Hull, J. W., & Appley, L. A. *Meeting today's responsibilities for tomorrow's managers.* Pasadena: Industrial Relations Center, California Institute of Technology, 1964.

Leigh, D. R. Development or developers. *Training and Development Journal,* 1966, *20*(10), 42–46.

Levinson, H. A psychologist looks at executive development. *Harvard Business Review,* 1962, *40(5), 69– 75.*

Miller, J. A., Haas, J. A., Bass, B. M., & Ryterband, E. C. *Exercise Future.* Pittsburgh, Pennsylvania: INSTAD, Ltd., 1970.

Schein, E. H. Management development as a process of influence. In H. J. Leavitt & L. R. Pondy (Eds.) *Readings in Managerial Psychology.* Chicago: University of Chicago Press, 1964. Pp. 331–351.

Vroom, V. H. *Work and motivation.* New York: Wiley, 1964.

# Mid-Career Education: Its Shape as a Function of Human Disequilibrium

R. M. Belbin   University College, London

There are few more pressing needs for those concerned with professional obsolescence than to establish something of the characteristics of the market for which mid-career education must cater. If education is to be provided it must be consumed. If we can establish some basic points about these potential consumers we can address ourselves the more readily to their requirements.

The facts of obsolescence in human skills and knowledge do not of themselves mean that pupils are awaiting further education. Only in the armed forces can people be drafted into classes and even here education consumption is more theoretical than real. Elsewhere mid-career education depends on voluntary enlistment.

The main parameters of this enlistment are well-established. Virtually all studies have shown the importance of age for attendance rates. As age increases smaller numbers present themselves for further education. For example a study by the Berkshire Education Authority in conjunction with Oxford University (Collie & Davis, 1968) shows that 21–45 is the predominant age group of students attending adult centres with only small numbers enrolled in the 50's. The same disinclination for older learners to present themselves is apparent from studies in vocational training. Government-sponsored training programmes are now being developed in about all the leading industrial countries of the world aimed especially at middle-age workers from declining industries who are now ripe for redeployment into the new expanding occupations. In the United Kingdom, the United States and Sweden where public policies have been directed with much vigour towards people of all ages the numbers of trainees over the age of 40 remains quite small and in other countries insignificant. In the private sector of industry the picture is much the same. During the course of the field experiments conducted by the Industrial Training Research Unit, we have had occasion to advertise on behalf of companies for middle-aged trainees. In many cases, in spite of shortage of job opportunities for older workers, or of local redundancies, the response has been very small. Many of those who did apply, opted out at the form-filling or selection test stage. Others chose to drift to jobs of lower skill or lower status where training would not be required. And relatively large numbers—relative, that is, to their younger colleagues—left during the early stages of training (Newsham, 1969).

The second major parameter governing the participation rate of middle-aged learners is that of social class. Even the Workers Educational Assocation, the name of which indicates the target population, has been found on examination to comprise a high proportion of middle-class members.

Allied to this phenomenon is our third parameter, that of educational status, competence and experience. Examination of the backgrounds of middle-aged participants in adult education has suggested that many of those who attend have either maintained a regular pattern of engaging in educational classes over a period of time, or they are attending for subjects in which they already hold some expertise (Frost, 1967). The importance of 'learning experience' as setting the stage for success in learning may underline this. In one study (Belbin & Waters, 1967) the causes of success and failure were investigated in a course of home study, supplemented by part-time tuition, for Coal Preparation examinees (see Table I).

TABLE I

AVERAGE EXAMINATION MARKS IN COAL PREPARATION COURSE
(in percent)

| | *Theory* | | *Practical* | |
|---|---|---|---|---|
| *AGE* | *"MAINTAINERS"* *(N=45)* | *OTHERS* *(N=44)* | *"MAINTAINERS"* | *OTHERS* |
| 20–29 | 71.3 | 53.6 | 72.3 | 72.9 |
| 30–39 | 71.5 | 57.0 | 74.5 | 75.9 |
| 40–49 | 69.4 | 53.1 | 75.8 | 71.5 |
| 50+ | 62.3 | 48.5 | 65.3 | 63.8 |

Those who had maintained some form of learning—whether it was First Aid, Art, Music, Wireless Telegraphy or Trade Union Law, did better in their Theory examination than the 44 who had attended no classes. In other respects such as schooling, job hierarchy or practical ability, their backgrounds were comparable.

Perhaps the most useful and comprehensive picture to emerge of the response of those in mid-career to opportunities for further education arises from applicants to the Open University. This is the body that had been sponsored by the Government to provide degree studies for part-time students, making use of television and radio programmes, supplemented by periodic tuition and counselling in regional study centres. The Open University provides an excellent means for the middle-aged aspirant with inadequate or obsolescence qualifications to upgrade himself. There are no formal qualifications for admission.

Tables II and III give an analysis of the first 30,000 applicants.

The most outstanding points of these tables are twofold: first, the high percentage of applicants who are already professionally involved in education—39.8%, if graduate teachers are also included—in comparison, say, with those from manual occupations: secondly, the moderately large proportions of applicants in the middle-age range even if these numbers diminish steadily from the 25–34 age group. Clearly, judging by the occupational breakdown many of these middle-aged applicants are engaged in jobs where a degree would offer scope for advancement.

This interpretation seems in line with the results of an international study of the factors conducive to effective retraining programmes in industry (Belbin, 1965). Many instances could be found of programmes that foundered through want of support and through the failure of trainees to progress. On the other hand some instances were found of outstanding successes in which members of the labour force covering a wide age span had completed a retraining course leading to more rewarding and demanding

## TABLE II

### APPLICANTS TO OPEN UNIVERSITY BY OCCUPATION

| Occupation Group | % of all applicants |
|---|---|
| Teachers | 37.4 |
| Professions and Arts | 10.6 |
| Housewives | 9.3 |
| Clerical and office staff | 7.5 |
| Draughtsmen, labaratory assistants and technicians | 6.4 |
| Administrators and managers | 6.2 |
| Qualified scientists and engineers | 6.1 |
| Graduates (in all other classes including 2.4% in teaching) | 4.5 |
| Shopkeepers, sales, services, sports, recreation workers, fire brigade and police | 3.1 |
| Not working (other than housewives), retired, independent means | 2.9 |
| Manufacturing (except as below), farming, mining, construction, transport and communications | 2.6 |
| Armed forces | 1.5 |
| Electrical, electronic, metal and welding and allied trades | 1.4 |
| Institutions, e.g. prisons | 0.2 |

## TABLE III

### APPLICANTS AS A PERCENTAGE OF THE AVAILABLE ADULT POPULATION IN GREAT BRITAIN BY AGE GROUPS

| Age: | 21–24 | 25–34 | 35–44 | 45–54 | 55–59 | 60–64 | 65 & over |
|---|---|---|---|---|---|---|---|
| | 1.13 | 1.77 | 1.28 | 0.70 | 0.20 | 0.09 | 0.03 |

jobs. The more successful schemes seemed to be characterised by group involvement and by real prospects of up-grading. An overview of the evidence reviewed so far suggests that there are two main groups of mature adults who are ready to present themselves for further education, these being: those who are professionally involved in education or who have continued to educate themselves throughout their adult lives as part of a general style, and those who see further education or retraining as a relevant means of self-advancement.

It is this second point which has perhaps so far received inadequate attention. Further education can be demonstrated as invaluable in assisting growth towards full human maturity and the economic goals which are an inseparable part of this maturity. But what similar part has further education to play for the mature and settled adult? We are led to hypothesise that only where some unsettling factor exists in the individual's equilibrium with his environment does continuing education become again a matter of personal urgency during middle and later maturity.

In expansion of this hypothesis we will need to distinguish between two sources of disequilibrium. The first we may regard as internal.

Recent research by Rapoport (1970) has highlighted the different patterns of development that follow an educationally-oriented course for senior British managers at the Administrative Staff College at Henley. The study was based on a questionnaire sent to those who had completed the course and which allowed for analysis of 287 variables. As a result of cluster analysis several types of manager could be identified. One group of managers appeared to develop by a process of steady growth: they saw Henley mainly as a provider of information. They gave answers to questions which on the cluster analysis showed them climbing, fulfilled and uncritical. This was termed an *incremental* pattern.

A contrasting group of respondents belonged to the *metamorphic* pattern of managerial development. These gave responses in creative-ambitious, venturesome, conflictful and restless-hard-driving categories. The metamorphic managers were easily dissatisfied with themselves and their environment. If they went to a university they tended to leave before completing their degrees yet enjoyed pre-Henley salary levels higher than those who did complete degrees, often tending to spiral upwards to better jobs in other firms if their employers offered them insufficient scope. Remarkably the metamorphics were the most enthusiastic about their experiences at Henley. They responded well to the more active exercises in learning, to the give-and-take of criticism and to the opportunities for rethinking their ideas about themselves and their relationship with others. The metamorphics show features of those who may profit most from further education (of the right type) in middle maturity. They combine a zest and natural capacity for achievement with a degree of immaturity and educational underdevelopment. It is through the very lack of self-realisation and sense of equilibrium with his environment that the metamorphic emerges as such promising material for further education.

The second source of urgency towards further education we must regard as external disequilibrium. This is brought about by changes in the individual's external world, over which he has very little control, and which creates for him a threat to his job role, his status, his life style and perhaps his very self-image. A man whose job has disappeared is faced not merely with the problem of learning another skill but of transforming himself in the process, almost of becoming a new man. The nature of this transformation can be better understood by examining the main sources of external disequilibrium. These are lateral transfer and job change, upgrading, demotion and early retirement.

## MAIN SOURCES OF EXTERNAL DISEQUILIBRIUM

### Lateral Transfer and Job Change

There are occasions when the refurbishing of skills presents more problems than retraining men for new jobs and careers. The reason is simply that if the basic essentials of a job change so radically that an individual's skill and knowledge are out-of-date, there is always a danger that he will be hindered by the persistence of outworn habits and attitudes, whereas transfer to a new job that embodies already developed component skills becomes a challenging and invigorating experience and one that opens up fresh educational horizons.

Most men's views of the future are largely circumscribed by what is possible. They expect to remain where they are or to get promoted, or if frustrated move to a similar position in another firm. this has been shown in Sofer's recent study of British managers and technical specialists (1970). Yet it is notable that a sizeable minority have aspirations of a job change. Of 81 respondents to a questionnaire 12 gave as their wishes for the future to 'stay in present firm but move department, try something new' and a further 6 would like to 'leave to try something new.' If provisions for further education and training made 'trying something new' more feasible, and the job opportunities existed, there seem grounds for believing that there would be plenty of people drawn from the middle ranks of management and the professions ready to explore the possibilities. The unblocking of promotion channels would be one of the attractions of such a development.

## Upgrading

Education and training with a view to promotion or upgrading is usually received with enthusiasm, perhaps because it is a stepping stone to better things. So, for example, junior and middle managers sent away to management courses usually report well of them and of what they have learned, although follow-up studies of changes in behaviour, other than transitory, have led to more sober assessment of their effectiveness. Behaviour is a long-term product both of an individual's personality and personal history and of the constraints imposed by the system in which he finds himself. An overview of the evidence suggests that further education and training gains greatest pay-off when an individual is about to enter into a new system. There fewer problems seem to arise by way of habitual response to stimulus variables of a familiar environment. The measure of disequilibrium rendered by the change of circumstances can be regarded as predisposing to the more fundamental impact which further education can bring to the individual.

## Demotion.

The prospect of demotion produces for an individual the greatest shock of all. Demotion is usually disguised—the salary remains the same, while another level is introduced above—or a person is shunted sideways into a non-job—but the message is unmistakeable.

It might be thought that nothing here can be done. But if our theory of the association between disequilibrium and further education is correct, it could be argued that this personal crisis will set the field for educational opportunity. In the Rapoport study there was evidence that one group of the managers were given fresh vistas by the educational process, gravitating away from preoccupation with the needs of the enterprise and becoming more aware of the opportunities of self-fulfilment and of enriching their life with their families. This group of individuals gave characteristic response clusters depicted as following a humanistic pattern of development. This group was characterised as comprising low scorers on the manipulative cluster of responses and high scorers on the accommodating. It seems likely that the role of education-cum-counselling has been insufficiently explored in the ways in which it could help an individual to reconcile himself to lower material and/or status prospects, yet to benefit from an enhanced richness of life.

## Early Retirement

Education for retirement has now become an acknowledged part of industrial education. Misgiving at the prospect of retirement seems greatest at some distance from it, say, about five years, and then recedes (Martin&Doran, 1964). Perhaps it is at the point of greatest shock that the best opportunities for further education lie. The most well received forms of education seem to be those aimed at retirement planning and while this is ostensibly concerned with straight forward matters of a practical nature, like building a greenhouse, there is a basic need for personal growth, for a new reorientation and adjustment towards what life has to offer.

## CONCLUSIONS

The theme of this paper then is that education and training in mid-career needs to be fashioned with great sensibility towards the characteristics of those who are to receive it. It is a matter of some importance to discover whether people are metamorphics, incremental or humanistic developers. But it is essential to discover the background of circumstances against which education and training now becomes a relevant activity. Are we fashioning our programmes for those who are moving towards well-defined goals, for those on the way up? Or are we fashioning a rescue operation for what Professor Page has described as the *competitive losers?* These are the people whose abilities and personality traits are not commensurate with the jobs they are currently performing. They are almost relieved to see and talk about themselves in frank terms without the need for pretence. Their orientation towards education and training seems to be characterised by a wish to capitalise on their assets and they judge the benefits of what they learn in concrete terms that are related to its bearing on their specific job and role.

A general conclusion then might be that for mid-career education to flourish account needs to be taken of the propensities of individuals as learners, of their prospects in employment, of the differences between their developed skills and those in need of cultivating and of the sources of disequilibrium generally that pronounce for continuing individual development.

The implications of these conclusions are first that there is much need of a diagnostician or counsellor to plan educational strategies for mature adult learners and secondly that the fullest use needs to be made of educational technology in tailoring training methods to suit particular types of people. The recent work of the Industrial Training Research Unit has identified 26 distinctive methods of training. In future those in mid-career no longer need contemplate education and training on a take-it-or-leave-it basis but will have options on the style, no less than on the subject, of the learning in which they wish to engage.

## REFERENCES

Belbin, E., Waters, P. Organised home study for older retrainees. *Industrial Training International*, May, 1967.

Belbin, R. M. Training methods. In series, *Employment of Older Workers*, O.E.C.D. Publications, Paris, 1965.

Collie, A., Davis, G. A survey of student attitudes.*Adult Education*, 1968, 139–147.

Frost, H. Residual mathematics in adults. Extra-mural Studies Occasional Papers, 1, University of London, 1967.

Martin, J., Doran, A. The perception of retirement. Unpublished monograph, Department of Psychology, Liverpool University, 1964.

Newsham, D. B. The challenge of change to the adult trainee. Training Information Pamphlet No. 3, HMSO, 1969.

Rapoport, R. N. Mid-career development: *Research perspectives in a developmental community for senior administrators*. London: Tavistock Publications, 1970.

Sofer, C. *Men in mid-career: A study of British managers and technical specialists*. Cambridge University Press, 1970.

# La Lutte Contre l'Obsolescence chez les Cadres Promus (Combatting Obsolescence in Promoted Managers)

**Robert Bosquet**     **l'Institut "Entreprise et Personnel"**
                       **Paris**

Dire de quelqu'un 'c'est un self made man' était, il y a peu de temps encore, un compliment. On évoquait ce faisant le dynamisme et la force vitale, le tempérament de lutteur, la jeunesse d'action. On craignait peut-être moins pour cet homme que pour un autre les risques d'obsolescence.

Aujourd'hui, le terme de cadre promu apparait dans de nombreux milieux comme un qualificatif d'infériorité. Le développement massif de l'enseignement supérieur, l'accroissement extraordinairement rapide des connaissances dans tous les domaines, ont modifié les termes de la comparaison. Les politiques d'embauche des entreprises le soulignent nettement, voir cruellement: le jeune diplômé est activement recherché; le cadre promu, plus âge, démuni de brillants diplômes, est le plus souvent considéré comme un candidat de seconde zône.

La formation, la rémunération, les méthodes modernes de direction sont orientées essentiellement vers ceux qui constituent un investissement pour l'entreprise: le cadre promu, le cadre sans formation universitaire, tend à être laissé à son devenir, à son obsolescence. Ce n'est donc pas une surprise de constater que ces cadres promus apparaissent deux à trois fois plus nombreux que les diplômés dans les statistiques de chômage, ou dans les 'laissés pour compte' lors des fusions, concentrations ou réorganisations.

Cette tendance est-elle fatale? Doit-on l'accepter tant du point de vue du développement de l'entreprise que de celle du devenir des hommes?

Ce sont ces deux questions que nous voudrions examiner.

## LES CARACTERISTIQUES SPECIFIQUES DES CADRES PROMUS

Il importe d'abord de rappeler quelles sont les caractéristiques spécifiques des cadres promus.

Les cadres promus sont souvent des hommes de caractère. Ils ont fait la preuve dans leur travail comme dans la recherche d'une formation complémentaire de leurs qualités de persévérance et de puissance de travail. Capables d'efforts importants, ils ont aussi tendance à travailler en force, dépensant davantage d'énergie qu'il n'est parfois nécessaire. Plus souvent hommes du concret (ils ont dû se confronter jeunes aux réalités. . . et ils ont été sélectionnés 'par le rejet' d'un enseignement plus orienté vers ceux qui possèdent des qualités d'intelligence abstraite et de généralisation), leur effort intellectuel est plus souvent un effort d'accumulation que de réelle assimilation des connaissances; ils veulent comprendre, mais ont besoin de temps; or celui-ci leur manque: leurs nouvelles connaissances risquent de rester à un stade superficiel, d'être insuffisamment assimilées pour être directement utilisables et se maintenir de façon durable. L'exigence d'un diplôme susceptible de leur ouvrir juridiquement le droit à une catégorie professionnelle supérieure peut les conduire à un 'bachotage,' peu conforme à leur personnalité et dangereux par l'impression de sécurité qu'il leur donne. Très conscients d'un manque de formation scientifique ou théorique, ils accordent en retour à celle-ci un prestige parfois excessif, ou tout au moins trop exclusif.

Riches d'expériences, ils sont aussi spécialisés. Cette spécialisation les pousse en avant dans la recherche d'une compétence; mais elle les polarise sur des secteurs assez étroits qui leur rend difficilement perceptible le besoin d'une culture personnelle plus large (celle-ci leur paraît moins utilisable en fait dans l'immédiat). Entre le court terme et le long terme, il y a une opposition qui ne leur apparaît que difficilement. L.hétérogénéité de leurs connaissances acquises en fonction de ces besoins immédiats, freine le développement d'une formation équilibrée. Aussi, s'ils n'ont pas eu l'occasion d'aborder plusieurs domaines professionnels, ou exercé des responsabilités humaines, leur spécialisation extrême les rend-elle peu sensibles aux activités et aux soucis des autres. Il est frappant de constater la corrélation entre le degré de spécialisation et le rejet des activités et responsabilités collectives; les difficultés dans les relations inter-services, dans la compréhension des objectifs économiques, financiers ou sociaux augmentent inéluctablement, malgré des qualités personnelles d'ouverture et de disponibilités souvent réelles, mais en quelque sorte paralysées.

L'expérience durement acquise a développé en eux le sens du possible et de la réalisation; ceci donne toute sa valeur à la notion de compromis, toujours plus proche de la solution pratique que en l'est la solution idéale satisfaisante pour l'esprit. En contrepartie, ce souci du compromis développe chez un grand nombre un conformisme certain (qui peut coexister paradoxalement avec un vif désir d'indépendance engendré par les réactions de défense ou les préoccupations égocentriques). Ce conformisme se manifeste entre autres par l'attirance qu'exerce sur eux les qualités de brillant qu'ils aperçoivent chez certains de leurs supérieurs: prestige de celui qui parle bien, de celui qui se comporte avec aisance, etc . . . Travaillant seuls, ils manquent pourtant de réelle autonomie. Ici aussi se manifeste un manque réel de culture générale.

Leur spécificité peut donc se marquer par ces quatre traits:
    des qualités de dynamisme, de volonté, d'accrochage,
    une expérience du concret, du possible pragmatique,
    une formation personnelle hétérogène, acquise par morceaux,
    un risque d'individualisme dû à l'intensité de l'effort personnel.

Ils ont en général été promus pour un poste donné et non pour occuper une famille de postes ou pour suivre une filière de carrière. Une promotion résulte donc le plus souvent d'une réponse à ou besoin immédiat. Rares sont les pays où les entreprises effectuent un effort important pour préparer les promus en fonction d'une échéance plus lointaine ou plus polyvalente. Des expériences remarquables comme la formation d'ingénieur en deux ans à temps plein donnée par le Centre d'Etudes Supérieures Industrielles à des hommes de 32-34 ans (en moyenne) sont rares. En général l'intéressé doit fournir un effort solitaire, ou ne bénéficie que de compléments sans comparaison avec la formation dont a bénéficié le jeune universitaire.

Il faut enfin souligner que la promotion a souvent entraîné pour le cadre un changement de milieu social. L'intégration plus ou moins réussie influera également sur l'obsolescence. De même l'adaptation sociale du conjoint et des enfants pèse sur le comportement et l'évolution future.

## LES RISQUES SPECIFIQUES D'OBSOLESCENCE

On conçoit facilement que les risques d'obsolescence sont plus grands pour les cadres promus. Mais cette obsolescence n'est pas homogène; aussi très souvent n'en perçoit-on pas aussi facilement l'arrivée, et surtout l'accélération.

Le vieillissement semblerait en effet connaitre une courbe d'accélération beaucoup plus marquée. La causeen serait double, tenant tant aux aptitudes intellectuelles qu'aux capacités d'adaptation sociale.

On sait parfaitement aujourd'hui que les aptitudes intellectuelles vieillissent régulière-ment, mais que ce vieillissement est très fortement limité par l'exercice régulier. Or très souvent, le cadre promu, homme du concret, n'ayant pas eu la possibilité de développer ses méthodes de travail intellectuel, manquant de culture générale, s'entraînera moins que les autres. Son goût pour la réalisation, voire pour des loisirs 'actifs,' n'aura pas suscité les mêmes curiosités, les mêmes besoins intellectuels. Il est ainsi plus vulnérable, tant du point de vue professionnel que personnel.

La spécialisation professionnelle fréquente des cadres promus renforce ce risque: plus forte est la spécialisation, plus fréquente semble la faiblesse de la culture personnelle. L'effort exigé pour se perfectionner verticalement est rarement (en Europe tout au moins) complétée par une ouverture horizontale. La moindre polyvalence d'adaptation qui en découle freine à son tour les possibilités de développement. C'est en quelque sorte le cercle vicieux: spécialisation→manque de culture générale et de polyvalence→ risque d'obsolescence naissant.

Accrochés au présent par leur esprit du concret, ces hommes sont moins aptes que les autres à penser dans l'avenir, à prévoir. Ils risquent donc de se laisser dépasser par l'évolution, tout particulièrement s'ils se trouvent dans un secteur de faible développement (ou en régression! ). Ils ont besoin d'être poussés au changement par leurs liens avec l'environnement; si celui-ci cesse de les stimuler, ils peuvent rapidement se cristalliser, voir diminuer rapidement leurs possibilités d'adaptation à d'autres tâches, à d'autres secteurs. Et c'est ainsi que l'on peut voir ces hommes, promus jadis pour leur dynamisme et leur sens de l'initiative réalisatrice, devenir des freins au progrès. Plus ce progrès revêtira des formes de connaissances générales et abstraites (connaissances scientifiques, économiques . . .), plus le blocage affectif risquera d'être accentué par le sentiment d'infériorité intellectuelle.

Cette inadaptation intellectuelle progressive risque malheureusement de ne pas être la seule. La même difficulté peut se présenter au plan social. Le cadre promu, qui a lutté pour arriver, qui n'a pas eu autant que les autres des possibilités de contact facile avec des milieux variés, risque de voir s'amplifier aves le temps cet écgocentrisme.

On constate cependant ici des évolutions très divergentes, dûes notamment à l'existence ou non d'activités sociales para ou extra-professionnelles. Leur volonté d'action conduit en effet un nombre important de cadres promus à participer aux activités collectives les plus diverses (sportives, de parents d'élèves, municipales, religieuses, syndicales . . .). Ce facteur externe est important dans le devenir du cadre promu: plus que le diplômé, son équilibre repose sur l'existence effective de ce triple support: vie professionnelle, vie familiale, vie sociale. Si l'effort professionnel est trop exclusif, les conséquences à long terme seront souvent sclérosantes.

On peut encore constater sur ce plan que le cadre promu n'est pas aussi soutenu par son milieu social que le cadre diplômé. Ayant en cours de carrière, changé souvent plusieurs fois de milieu, il n'est pas aussi intégré. Son conjoint et ses enfants n'ont pas toujours évolué au même rythme. Les risques de dysharmonies sont plus nombreux. Cela peut conduire à des difficultés crossantes d'adaptation pyscho-sociologique.

Efin signalone cette tentation chez le promu du brillant, de la forme en soi. Ce prestige de 'celui qui parle bien,' qui s'adapte facilement à la société peut conduire à la recherche d'un vernis culturel et social qui ne résiste pas au temps. Mal intégré à la personnalité, il ne s'auto-développe pas . . . et vieillit donc mal.

## LES MOYENS A METTRE EN OEUVRE

Toutes les observations que nous venons de rapporter montrent de façon concordante la nécessité pour le promu d'acquérir une formation personnelle au cours de sa carrière. C'est en effet essentiel . . . Mais à condition de ne confondre formation, ni avec acquisition de connaissances, ni avec obtention de diplômes! Le terme doit être pris à son sens le plus large, celui de développement:

*des* connaissances, de l'expérience, de l'efficience intellectuelle, des aptitudes personnelles, de l'équilibre physique et nerveux

*par* la carrière, le travail quotidien, les responsabilités familiales et sociales, les loisirs . . .

C'est en fait d'une capacité d'auto-développement en relation et en fonction du milieu ambiant le plus large que le cadre promu a besoin. Là se trouve le noeud de la lutte ultérieure contre le vieillissement.

—Les connaissances bénéficient toujours d'une place de choix dès qu'il s'agit de promotion. Très souvent, la porte s'ouvre sur les résultats d'un examen. La hiérarchie professionnelle (et sociale)tenden effet de plus en plus à se rapprocher de la hiérarchie scolaire et universitaire: c'est le certificat d'aptitude du Professionnel, le diplôme du technicien ou de l'ingénieur, etc. Ceci explique l'intense effort effectué actuellement pour permettre l'acquisition de ces connaissances aux adultes: réalisations de l'Education Nationale, de Ministère des Affaires Sociales, des organisations professionnelles, des entreprises, des collectivités locales . . .

Cette recherche de connaissances mérite cependant d'être entreprise avec prudence: elle représente en effet des efforts de longue durée (chaque échelon professionnel correspond à plusieurs années d'études effectuées dans le processus scolaire normal à temps plein); elle représente aussi un prestige traditionnel au sein de notre société, prestige qui tend parfois à faire acquérir un diplôme donc des connaissances dont il n'est pas toujours besoin.

Les connaissances ne doivent donc pas être surestimées par rapport aux autres élements de le promotion . . . et surtout ne pas être recherchées uniquement en elles-mêmes, indépendamment de l'orientation personnelle et professionnelle. L'effort à consentir risquerait en effet alors d'être si grand . . . qu'il serait pratiquement très difficile à réaliser et sacrifierait les autres facteurs de réussite.

—Le manque d'expérience est souvent plus grave que le manque de connaissances . . . parced que moins visible, particulièrement en ce qui concerne la compétence humaine: direction des hommes, méthodes de travail et comportement . . . A partir de certains échelons hiérarchiques, il est même patent que l'expérience conditionne l'assimiliation réelle des connaissances (l'accroissement d'expérience permet l'acquisition de nouvelles connaissances, qui permettent à leur tour l'acquisition de nouvelles expériences, et ainsi de suite . . .)

L'expérience vaut par la compétence, mais surtout par l'adaptabilité qu' elle donne. Elle doit être vue comme une part intégrante de la culture générale. L'expérience ne peut se valoriser dans un seul poste, une seule fonction, une seule entreprise. Elle doit être ouverture sur des milieux différents: technique, de gestion, humain . . . elle doit être capacité de responsabilité future dans des situations, avec des personnes, différentes de celles d'aujourd'hui. Trop de cadres aujourd'hui en chômage sont en fait les victimes d'une expérience trop spécialisée, trop focalisée pourrait-on dire; il n'y a pas eu valorisation.

—L'efficience intellectuelle dépendra souvent et de la diversification de la carrière, et d'une ouverture permanente sur une formation générale. Il est possible d'être intelligent et peu cultivé; il ne l'est guère d'être efficace intellectuellement sans réelle culture. C'est dire qu'un effort de promotion ne peut être axé uniquement sur une orientation professionnelle au sens étroit du terme et que toute spécialisation même couronnée de succès dans l'immédiat risque fort de créer des difficultés d'adaptation à terme. Tout le problème de l'emploi est remis en cause par cette constation.

—Le développement de la personnalité des cadres promus doit s'effectuer dans le double sens d'une autonomie et d'une faculté d'adaptation au milieu croissantes. L'autonomie favorisera le développement du potentiel propre du promu; l'adaptation au milieu facilitera les échanges 'moi-monde' nécessaires au progrès personnel. Plus encore que pour les cadres diplômés, les responsabilités sur les autres, la direction du travail d'autrui constituent le plus précieux atout de développement personnel. Le cadre promu a besoin de cette confrontation, de ces tensions avec les autres pour obtenir sa propre valorisation. Les rapports entre le travail et l'équilibre personnel sont également touchés par l'action conjuguée du développement culturel et spirituel et de ses conséquences sur le rythme physiologique. Le développement culturel doit normalement augmenter l'efficience professionnelle. Il entraîne à terme une promotion du travail. Mais l'homme, donnant plus, exige aussi plus. Il recherche, dans la fonction qu'il occupe, son propre épanouissement. Elargissant son champ de compétences et ses ouvertures, il acquiert davantage d'autonomie.

Il semble bien qu'il y ait deux périodes-clés pour le perfectionnement général des cadres promus en cours de carrière. L'une peut être située vers 30/35 ans pour ceux qui se sont révélés capables de recevoir une promotion rapide vers la catégorie supérieure. L'autre sera entre 40 et 50 ans soit pour des hommes dont la promotion a été plus lente ou plus faible, soit pour d'autres qui doivent à ce moment connaître une véritable reconversion professionnelle. A cette situation doit correspondre un nouveau démarrage et une nouvelle capacité d'adaptation aux problèmes et aux personnes.

Mais cette formation doit être conçue essentiellement comme un adjuvant, un moyen de valoriser la carrière professionnelle (et l'adaptation familiale et sociale qu'il importe de ne pas oublier): plus que les diplômés, les cadres promus ont besoin d'un plan de carrière, les préparant à une suffisante polyvalence, leur facilitant des passerelles entre différentes fonctions (à l'inverse les intéressés doivent comprendre que ces mutations de postes ne peuvent se faire avec des promotions automatiques! ).

## QUI EST RESPONSABLE DE CETTE LUTTE?

La lutte contre l'obsolescence chez les cadres promus ne peut s'effectuer favorablement que par l'action conjuguée de 3 séries de partenaires: les intéressés, les entreprises et les pouvoirs publics.

Les intéressés sont naturellement les acteurs essentiels dans cette action. Il leur faut à la fois une lucidité suffisante sur eux-mêmes, une connaissance du développement et du vieillissement de la personne, un soutien familial et une volonté persévérante. Mais ils ne peuvent souvent lutter efficacement sans une action concertée, notamment au sein de l'entreprise. Les responsables hiérarchiques ont ici une responsabilité essentielle. Les difficultés ne se présentent en effet pas seulement aux niveaux des structures nationales, mais aussi, et surtout peut-être, au niveau des contraintes quotidiennes: les exigences de le production, du rendement; le manque de temps, de disponibilité; les habitudes de chaque jour . . . Ce sont ces difficultés de chaque instant qui devront être dépassées pour faire admettre le besoin, susciter les possibilités de réalisation. Tant que le désir de formation continue—un désir adapté aux besoins professionnels—ne représentera pas une exigence d'emploi dûment motivée, les efforts de promotion et de perfectionnement ne trouveront pas leur place. C'est à ce niveau que se situe essentiellement la responsabilité des cadres.

Cette responsabilité n'exclut naturellement pas celle des pouvoirs publics ou celle des organisation professionnelles (qu'elles soient d'employeurs ou de salariés). Ces deux responsabilités ne sont simplement pas de même nature. Pouvoirs publics et organisations professionnelles ont pour mission d'analyser statistiquement les besoins, de prévoir le cadre institutionnel de la formation, de faire procéder aux recherche pédagogiques nécessaires, d'informer et d'inciter les intéressés et les employeurs (psychologiquement et financièrement). Cette tâche en elle-même est énorme; son énormité explique en partie les difficultés que rencontre la 'mise au monde' de la formation continue, alors que la formation des jeunes est également en profonde mutation et mobilise et les attentions et les fonds. Les interférences politiques viennent compliquer encore le problème; l'éducation a toujours été un des leviers de modification de la société et un des arguments électoraux auxquels la population est normalement sensible. Ces interférences sont justifiées certes; il importe cependant de ne pas céder à la tentation de faciles oppositions: l'intérêt des groupes à court terme ne correspond pas nécessairement à l'intérêt de la collectivité à long term. Donner à la moitié ou même au tiers de la population scolarisable une formation égale ou supérieure à la licence ne serait pas, quelle que soit la valeur de l'enseignement supérieur, le moyen le plus réaliste pour améliorer le sort de chacun. Réserver cette même formation à une soi-disant élite est aussi choquant pour l'intérêt général! Dans les deux cas le problème est faussé dès le départ.

Cette responsabilité des hiérarchiques correspond à des fonctions multiples: orienter leurs collaborateurs, aménager les fonctions et objectifs, dégager du temps pour la formation, obtenir des moyens financiers, conseiller dans le travail et aider au perfectionnement sur le tas, faire évaluer les résultats . . . et donner l'exemple! Cette multiplicité souligne que cette action des supérieurs doit elle-même se placer dans le cadre d'une action collective cohérente. Une telle responsabilité ne peut être laissée à la bonne volonté individuelle sous peine de se restreindre progressivement.

## LES PERSPECTIVES

L'évolution économique et sociale des années à venir ne facilitera sans doute pas l'adaptation spontanée des cadres promus et leur lutte contre l'obsolescence. Les agressions et les contraintes nouvelles risqueront au contraire de conduire à des désadaptations et à une obsolescence plus rapide, si l'on en croit les experts du groupe 'Reflexions pour 1985."[1] :

'Sur le plan de son comportement psychologique et social, l'homme de 1985 sera menacé d'une moindre adaptation psychologique et sociale . . . il sera soumis à de nouvelles contraintes et à de nouvelles dépendances; entraîne par des modèles qui lui sont suggéres de façon contraignante plus que par la valeur d'usage des biens; pris dans la hiérarchie des revenus, des métiers, des modes de possession; déterminé dans ses délassements, ses loisirs, sa vie culturelle, par la nature des équipements collectifs qui existeront . . . La vie s'accordant de moins en moin directement aux rythmes bio-logiques et naturels (climats artificiels, urbanisation de la campagne quant à l'apparence de l'habitat et au mode de vie . . .) l'obligation de se mouvoir dans un espace artificiellement construit et restreint, amèneront l'individu à perdre progressive-ment son autonomie individuelle . . ."

On conçoit facilement quel'homme en promotion—qui connait une accélération de l'évolution dans tous les domaines: capacités professionnelles, responsabilités sociales, exigences culturelles, vie familiale, mode de vie et statut social . . .—soit particulière-ment touché par cette transformation profonde du milieu dans lequel nous vivrons dans les années à venir. L'adaptation est pour cet homme plus importante que pour un autre; il lui faut donc davantage de moyens, davantage de volonté, davantage de capacités. Nous avons tendu à souligner la responsabilité qu'avait la collectivité tout entière de donner à ces hommes la formation générale et humaine nécessaire à leur épanouissement—comme à l'acquisition d'une véritable compétence professionnelle—. Nous avons vu qu'actuellement ces moyens n'existaient que rarement. Cest hommes, qui constituent une des élites de la collectivité parce qu'ils sont moteurs de changment et de progrès, parce qu'ils se sentent capables de rendre davantage, ces hommes sont souvent abandonnés à eux-mêmes faute de temps, faute de moyens, faute aussi d'imagination fáce aux structures et aux habitudes actuelles.

Cette priorité du rendement immédiat face aux difficultés prévisibles de l'avenir met en péril la promotion sociale toute entière telle qu'elle est conçue aujourd'hui. Elle met en péril tout individu qui ne saura par ses propres moyens essentiellement surmonter ces difficultés et s'adapter à cette double évolution 'd'un homme qui doit changer dans un monde qui change.' Elle le condamne en fait à vieillir plus mal et plus vite.

En ce sens la lutte contre l'obsolescence des cadres promus sera un test: celui du développement réel de la formation permanente et de son efficacité pour l'épanouis-sement personnel et professionnel des hommes.

---

[1] groupe de hautes personnalités chargées par le gouvernement français en 1963 de rechercher le sens de l'évolution de la société dans les 20 années à venir.

# Updating in the Royal Air Forces Training

**Gilbert Jessup**     **Ministry of Defence,**
**United Kingdom**

The Services have been experiencing the problems of retraining people for rapidly changing job situations for many years. Some of the ways in which the Services have coped with the situation and some implications for the careers of professional officers are discussed in this paper.

There are two main reasons why an individual's job changes rapidly in the Armed Services. First, the equipment becomes obsolete and new equipment is introduced at a rate exceeding that of most British industrial organisations. For example, Royal Air Force squadrons undergo a complete re-equipment of aircraft and ancillary equipment about every ten years. Also during the life of an aircraft very substantial modifications to it takes place sometimes amounting to a complete change of equipment inside the airframe throughout the life of the aircraft. The second factor causing job change is the system of job rotation common in the Armed Services. In the Royal Air Force, for example, job rotation is based on a two and half year cycle. Officers and airmen typically change both their jobs and the location of their jobs every two to three years. The aim of job rotation is to provide both wide experience, considered to be necessary for the more senior posts, and to provide flexibility for posting men from one job to another at short notice.

An additional consideration is that the nature of an officer's job changes throughout his career as he gains in seniority. For example, the General Duties officer in the RAF spends most of the first half of his career on flying duties and most of the second half in management and administration. Figure 1 outlines the career of a senior General Duties officer who is still serving in the Royal Air Force.

Each box represents a separate tour, a position or job occupied by a man. This officer's first three tours were on flying, followed by a mixed period in mid-career. Then he was assigned to eight tours in command staff posts, the last three of which were all staff. During this period the officer was promoted from Pilot Officer to Air Commodore (one star general).

Examples will be drawn primarily from career studies carried out in the Royal Air Force. Each officer is trained and works within a particular branch or professional category and each airman is trained in a trade. Since conscription has not existed for ten years in Great Britain, short service commissions are uncommon in the Royal Air Force. The large majority of officers are career personnel and the training pattern is designed accordingly.

It might be argued that in peace time the only function of an armed service is to train. This is certainly not the way it is perceived by the services themselves or the Treasury.

**Figure 1. THE CAREER OF A GENERAL DUTIES PILOT**

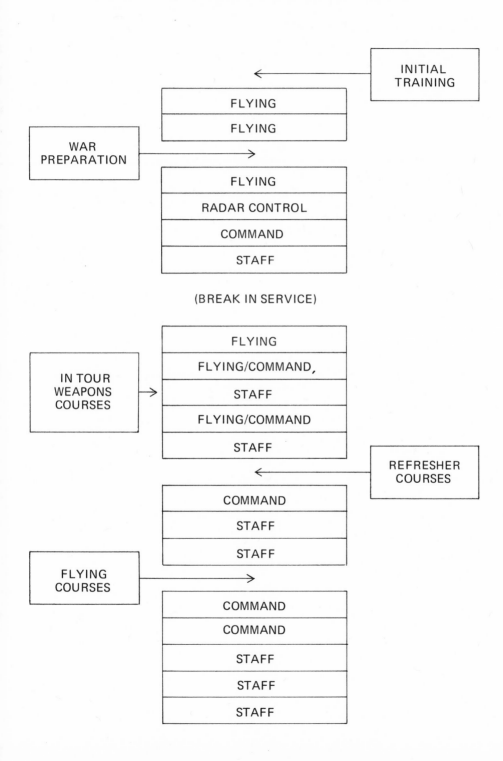

The training described in this paper is formal training on full-time courses in training establishments. A clear distinction is perceived between this and working on operational units. Formal training is very costly and the cost of each course must be justified in terms of the contribution it makes to increased efficiency. Formal training also takes men out of operational service which in time of manning shortages places considerable strain on operational units.

Initial training in the RAF, apart from general service training, provides a general professional or trade training. Engineers obtain training in engineering, mechanical or electrical, up to about university level plus training in service applications. Many officers go to universities as part of their initial training and obtain degrees; others are awarded degrees at the Royal Air Force College Cranwell. In addition to this broad initial training engineers undergo a number of advanced and specialist courses.

An officer's training can be divided into two progressive ladders: the general administrative and management training which all career officers follow and the specialist professional training which is peculiar to each branch. The general ladder (Figure 2) shows the volume and sequential nature of officer training.

### Figure 2   GENERAL OFFICER TRAINING

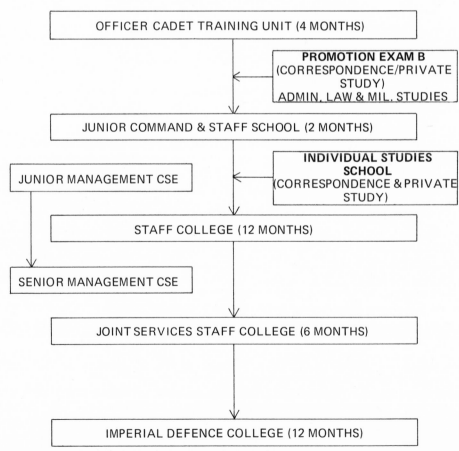

**Figure 3** **SPECIALIST/PROFESSIONAL TRAINING FOR ENGINEER OFFICERS**

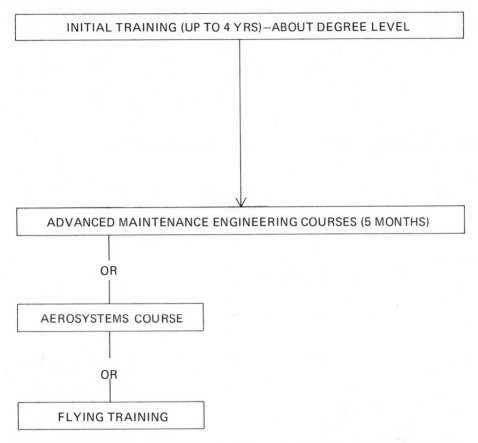

| INITIAL TRAINING (UP TO 4 YRS) – ABOUT DEGREE LEVEL |

| ADVANCED MAINTENANCE ENGINEERING COURSES (5 MONTHS) |

OR

| AEROSYSTEMS COURSE |

OR

| FLYING TRAINING |

PLUS MANY SHORT COURSES ON SPECIALIST EQUIPMENTS, COMPUTERS ETC. AND EXTERNAL COURSES

Although only a small minority of officers complete the whole sequence the majority go some way up the ladder.

The sequence of specialist training for engineer officers is shown in Figure 3.

Apart from the initial training and one of the advanced courses, further training of engineers is mainly a matter of individual requirements depending upon the job he is to take up.

One of the specific forms of up-dating employed in the RAF is 'conversion training.' When changing from one type of aircraft to another pilots typically undergo conversion training. Pilots commonly take several such conversion courses during their career. An example of a pilot's career showing the conversion courses undertaken is shown in Figure 4.

**Figure 4    GENERAL DUTIES OFFICER'S CAREER—1**

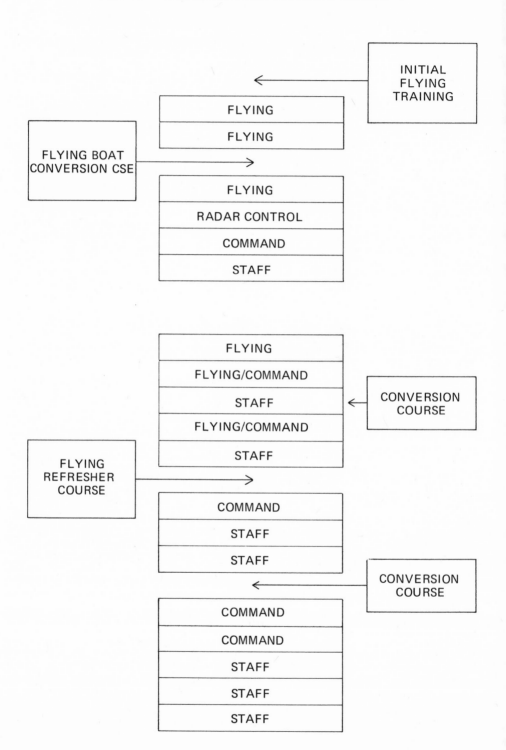

## Figure 5 ENGINEER OFFICER'S CAREER—1

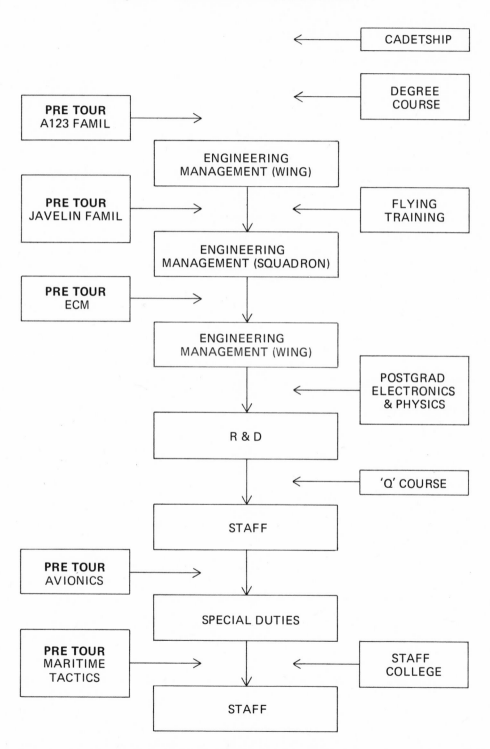

A second form of up-dating common in the RAF is pre-tour training. This occurs when the job requirements of the next tour to which an officer is posted specify skills and knowledge outside his repertoire. He then goes on specific short courses to rectify this deficit. Examples are shown in Figure 5.

In addition to pre-tour and conversion courses, various professional journals such as *Air Clues,* educational bulletins and other written communications are circulated to keep people informed of new developments in equipment, discoveries about performance defects in equipment and new techniques. Apart from service organised training officers are encouraged to pursue external courses at local universities and technical colleges. Officers often take external management courses, obtain professional qualifications within their specialisation and occasionally obtain higher degrees.

The ideal training/career pattern would be such that for every job the training plus experience requirements are specified. Officers would be allocated to posts according to suitability in respect of these requirements with the additional topping-up of training to bring them up to the standard required. But there are additional considerations to take into account in allocating posts, such as providing varied experience to equip officers to hold senior posts. The compromise between these two objectives—that is allocating the best man to the job and maximising efficiency in the short run or providing men with experience to maximise efficiency in the senior posts—represents the major problem which career planners face. The fact that engineer officers themselves are divided on this issue was shown in a recent career study of Engineers carried out in the Royal Air Force.[1]

The study was based primarily on 751 completed questionnaires which provided detailed information on the careers, training and work attitudes of engineer officers. In this survey 42% thought that the Engineer Branch would be more efficient if there was more specialisation, the result of posting officers to the jobs for which they are best qualified. On the other hand, 58% thought the general and varied career maximised the overall efficiency of the branch.

In this study engineer officers' jobs were classified in six categories: Engineering Management (Squadron), Engineering Management (Wing), Research and Development, Staff (MOD), Staff (Command), Instruction.

Engineering management is the predominant activity of junior officers while staff work or administration is the main activity of senior officers. A typical officer's career is illustrated in Figure 6.

The transition from specialist activity towards management and administration is of course the normal pattern in many organisations; the training received by this officer throughout his career also reflects the change of function.

Our study showed that the type of job officers felt best qualified to perform also changes in the expected direction though not sufficiently to represent the true allocation of posts at each level.

Preferences among engineer officers for different types of work also changes throughout a career, as can be seen in Figure 7.

---

[1]  Levene & Jessup, 1970

**Figure 6 ENGINEER OFFICER'S CAREER—2**

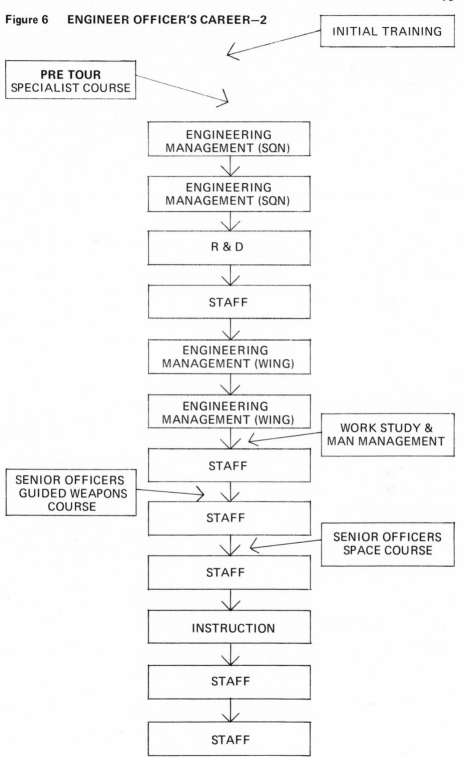

94

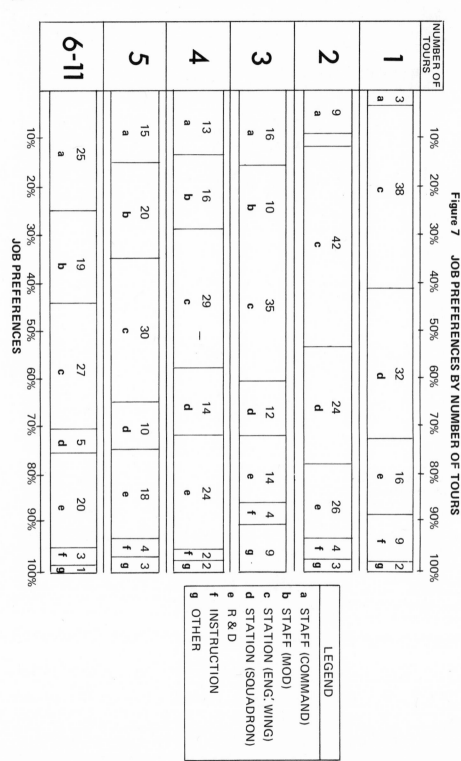

Figure 7   JOB PREFERENCES BY NUMBER OF TOURS

| NUMBER OF TOURS | | 10% | 20% | 30% | 40% | 50% | 60% | 70% | 80% | 90% | 100% |
|---|---|---|---|---|---|---|---|---|---|---|---|
| 1 | 3 a | 38 c | | | 32 d | | 16 e | | 9 f | 3 g | 2 |
| 2 | 9 a | 42 c | | | 24 d | | 26 e | | 4 f | 3 g | |
| 3 | 16 a | 10 b | 35 c | | 12 d | | 14 e | | 4 f | 9 g | |
| 4 | 13 a | 16 b | 29 c | — | 14 d | | 5 d | 18 e | 2 f | 2 g | |
| 5 | 15 a | 20 b | 19 b | 30 c | 27 c | | 10 d | 18 e | 20 e | 4 f | 3 g |
| 6-11 | 25 a | 19 b | | 27 c | | | 5 d | 20 e | 3 f | 1 g | |

JOB PREFERENCES

LEGEND

a  STAFF (COMMAND)
b  STAFF (MOD)
c  STATION (ENG: WING)
d  STATION (SQUADRON)
e  R & D
f  INSTRUCTION
g  OTHER

### Figure 8    JOB SATISFACTION BY TYPE OF WORK

| JOB CATEGORY | JOB SATISFACTION | | | |
|---|---|---|---|---|
| | HIGH | INTER | LOW | Nos IN SAMPLE |
| STATION (SQN) | 78.1 | 20.7 | 1.2 | 82 |
| R & D | 68.9 | 25.4 | 5.7 | 157 |
| STATION (ENG WG) | 63.3 | 26.3 | 10.4 | 289 |
| STAFF (MOD) | 46.3 | 32.4 | 21.3 | 80 |
| STAFF (COMMAND) | 40.9 | 31.8 | 27.3 | 66 |
| INSTRUCTION | 40.1 | 49.3 | 10.6 | 35 |
| | | | | |
| OTHER | 59.2 | 26.7 | 14.1 | 71 |

Figure 8 shows the extent of job satisfaction expressed by officers occupying posts in the different categories.

An assessment was made of the degree of identification or allegiance professionals have with their organisation and with their profession. The question asked was:
  Do you think of yourself as
    An Engineer first, Officer second ..........
    An Officer first, Engineer second ..........

The response indicates the degree of professionalism which exists in the engineering branch of the RAF. Among the engineers the result was as follows: 63% replied that they considered themselves engineers first; 25% considered themselves officers first.

A further finding was that officers who considered themselves officers first were somewhat more satisfied with service life as a whole (75%) than officers who considered themselves engineers first (62%). This attitude may influence an officer's decision to stay or leave the service at their mid-career option point.

Finally, some of the problems connected with the resettlement of officers in civilian life must be considered. In a recent study in the UK a questionnaire was sent to a sample of 5,400 officers who had left the Army, Royal Navy and Royal Air Force during the previous three years. Ninety-four percent wanted further employment and 90% actually took up further employment. A large number of these officers were in their thirties and forties. Also, 40% of those who had completed a full career in the services and were in their fifties also took further employment. The findings indicate that the majority of officers leaving the service embark on a serious second career. The professionally qualified officers take up civilian jobs within their profession and although the adjustment and retraining process can be considerable their problems are fewer than those without recognisable qualifications. The latter often start on a completely fresh career in a different field in the middle of their working life. These examples are of particular relevance to those studying professional obsolescence.

The categories of initial employment undertaken by officers leaving the service were: professional (27%), administrative/management (10%), clerical (33%), sales (12%), transport/communications (8%), sport/recreation (4%), others (6%).

The large number in the clerical category is made up chiefly of those leaving the service over the age of 50 years. Pilots who continued flying are included in the transport category. The factors which determine the occupational category chosen by an officer appears to be branch of service, the service itself, rank and age of leaving, in that order. A breakdown of the 27% of officers entering professional employment shows that the initial jobs taken were in the following occupational categories: school teaching (34%); engineering (20%); university/technical college lecturers (13%); other technological work (12%); accounts, company secretaries, registrars (6%); authors, journalism (4%); social welfare work (4%); medicine (2%); . . . Nearly half of the officers in this group (47%) take up teaching and about another third pursue engineering (including the 'technological workers'). Finally, in relation to the resettlement study, it is worth noting that the large majority of officers who leave the service express satisfaction with their new jobs: 48% indicated that they were very satisfied; 39%, fairly satisfied. The remaining 13% were either indifferent or dissatisfied.

In the context of professional obsolescence it would be perhaps worth-while sponsoring a detailed study of the transition from service to civilian life experienced by service officers. I would hypothesize that men in middle life who had experienced the regular job changes and continual up-dating as have service officers are more flexible and better able to embark on a second career compared to men of comparable ability who had followed a less varied career. That is to say, I would expect up-dating and retraining to be most successful among people who have experienced regular changes in their career and who have come to expect change in the future. The resettlement of officers presents a situation where it might be feasible to test the hypothesis.

# Updating Management Practices in Italy

**G. Martinoli**    **Italian National Council of Research,**
**Milan**

As an industrial manager for almost forty years, my knowledge of the problems of education, training and professional obsolescence has been obtained on the industrial side of the barricade. I have spent all my life as a 'consumer' of the 'products' of education.

My experience, furthermore, is limited to the Italian industrial situation. The organizational level of most of the industrial companies of Italy would appear to be inferior to that generally reached by large American firms.[1] This fact is mainly due to the different nature and conception of management and organization in Italy, compared with U.S.A. and many other countries of less recent economic development. Even if the leadership level of some Italian industrial companies is satisfactory and the organization structure acceptable, we must admit that top management's attitude is, for some aspects, still feudal; most organizational structures are elemenatry, confused and rough. The delegation of responsibilities, the administrative decentralization, the severance of tasks according to specific functions and specializations, the accurate planning of future activities in general are not commonly adopted and rigidly observed by our managers. Relations with personnel are often poor, and inspection is often confused with espionage.

We do not lack publications and books—original or translated—in which the concepts and the principles of a modern, rational, advanced management are illustrated in a clear and precise way. We do not lack courses for the training and development of managers or even for middle-managers and supervisors. There are many Italian or foreign consultants who are able to assist our enterprises and to transfer managerial experiences and their results from the most advanced American industrial companies.

However, the importance of continuing education of personnel, of integrating post-experience capability with formal education, of improving knowledge both in technology and in organization, is mainly ignored, undervalued or not understood by many Italian industrialists and managers, even among those who have obtained a fair success in their business. Italian industrialists, often founders of industrial enterprises,

---

[1] Dr. Dubin sent me the *Highlights* of his studies: 'A Survey of Continuing Professional Education Needs for Engineers in Pennsylvania' and 'Management and Supervisory Educational Needs of Business and Industry in Pennsylvania,' to assist me in preparing my paper. When I received them I must confess that I was frightened and disheartened. The precision of terms employed; of the classification in categories and levels of managers, middle-managers, first-line supervisors; of the list of educational requirements and of subject areas used in the questionnaire for which people require better information, have induced me to remark that if someone should proceed to similar investigations in my country, he would gather poor, confused, deceiving and mostly useless data.

and Italian managers of many of our companies often attend conventions, round tables, national and international symposia, where these problems are examined and discussed. They lavish enthusiastic praise on concepts and principles that in the daily administration of their factories are disregarded or are considered as pure theoretical abstractions.

Thereafter however, retraining and promotion on the job of the personnel do not exceed the threshold of good intentions. It is difficult and rare to obtain changes in the attitude of the managers with regard to the environment in which they are supposed to operate.

In fact, many top managers are fairly disposed to introduce rationality into the structures of their companies and in the methods of administration and control, but only on condition that this does not take away anything from their privileges, that it does not encroach on their mainly autocratic and dictatorial conception of leadership. According to this attitude, the top manager, the owner of a company, is willing to use only the executive abilities of his managers, rejecting the contribution they could make to the company through new ideas, new initiatives and interesting innovations. The typical Italian top manager is generally convinced that he is always right and that he always acts in the right way. When he does delegate some responsibility, and perhaps in good faith he does not entirely trust the chosen delegate, but often wants to intervene in order to assess whether the decisions taken are 'right' or 'wrong.'

I beg your indulgence for this long description. It may appear pessimistic and exaggerated to one who is aware of the undeniable successes obtained internationally by Italian industry in some sectors—automobiles, home appliances, office equipment, attire, fashion and cinema. However, I would like to mention that this picture is not exclusive to our country. Possibly, in other countries, and even in the United States of America there are to be found many situations to which the above mentioned description corresponds pretty faithfully.

Taking such situations of organizational climate into account, the environment of each company must be fully examined when we want to improve the qualification of the personnel, to update their professional training. In fact, where situations of this nature dominate, where the management is close-minded, where there is no reciprocal confidence, the possibility of improving the qualification of personnel is difficult if not nonexistent. Perhaps my past experience in different industrial companies has given me a particular sensitivity and awareness of the gap existing between the programs, plans, the prescriptions furnished by the management and their actual realization. My experience puts me in a position to evaluate and assess how far we are from neat theoretical models.

## MANAGEMENT – ITALIAN STYLE

Perhaps many teachers do not feel the depth and the breadth of the gap that still exists between scholastic education, especially at the university level, and the cultural average level of a majority of the managers and leaders, in Italy as well as in many other countries. It is with the consciousness of this gap that we must consider the possibilities of education within the company.

It is worthwhile mentioning that the cultural level of Italian managers and industrialists is, generally speaking, modest. Statistics published by O.C.D.E. (DAS/EID/68.36 — Direction des Affaires Scientifiques — Formation et Utilisation du Personnel Hautement Qualifié) indicate that only 7.2% of the 'grands patrons' and 28.5% of the administrative managers of big industries in France have a university degree—and the Italian situation is certainly worse. In any case, we should also ask ourselves if the type of university education is really suitable to prepare managers. They are, or should be, men with a strong spirit of initiative and innovation who like to take risks and therefore who are not conformist, men full of fantasy and creativeness. The university education is probably more adequate for high level technicians, for bureaucrats, for teachers, that is to say for men more inclined to reflection than to action.

In order to understand the difficulty in introducing sound educational concepts into the structure of an industrial company, we must recognize that in the mind of the ordinary Italian manager, the self-made man, education is very often identified with the kind of education he has received in his childhood, in which there was an unforgettable relationship with an authoritarian teacher, who, ex cathedra, forced upon students notions and concepts already elaborated, manipulated, and fully digested. Moreover, to the Aristotelian-deductive type of education, still prevailing in Latin and German countries, in contrast with the pragmatic one prevailing in the Anglo-Saxon countries, we owe that difference of attitude, at a managerial level, that may perhaps explain also the differences existing in the economic sphere.

Our remarks are of course more applicable to the small and medium-sized companies which absorb 75—80% of the workers of Italian industry. Most of their owners and managers rise from the ranks. The ascent of simple workers and foremen from the most modest and humble tasks to more ambitious ones, and even to the top management, should be considered as an educational process of great pedagogical importance. However, the efficiency of this process is lost for the worker of average ability and evident only in the case of individuals with conspicuous inborn endowments, and therefore quite rare. Whether we rely on intrinsic endowments of a few individuals or on occasional opportunities offered to them by chance, many opportunities are lost for a better development of the human resources of society. In particular, individuals whose native abilities are not apparent from the beginning may be overlooked; suitable educational programs could develop their talents if they were recognized.

In larger companies, the figure of the entrepreneur, the initial founder of their fortunes—generally an undisguised autocrat, a typical individual of an early industrialization age—is tending now to disappear even from our country. Little by little, the top authority is delegated to the president and to the board of directors. In these companies, the personnel with managerial functions and even middle-managers, are recruited now from among people with university degrees, so that the characteristics and nature of the management environment tend to change gradually. However, this evolution is more evident in the offices than in the line and in the factories, where only today some young men with a secondary education (thirteen years attendance at school, of which the last five years have a specific technical nature), are promoted as foremen or supervisors. This trend is at least more evident now than in the past. Yet the total replacement in the middle and top management of old individuals coming from the ranks will still require many years, and the influence of self-made men will be felt for a long time in our companies. One must not undervalue also the circumstance that many self-made entrepreneurs and managers, with a low level education, generally mistrust and avoid hiring individuals with higher education. In environments of this nature and in accordance with this kind of mentality, promotion on the job does not take place by merit and intrinsic capacity of the individual, but it is tied to a loyalty to the company or to the boss who personifies it. In many cases the management trusts the executives who prove to be harsh to their co-workers and able to impose on them a substantially formal discipline.

## CURRENT TRAINING METHODS

Foremen having such educational background are supposed to perform all the tasks related to the nine functions, which, according to Taylor and to the best criteria for a rational organization, should be accomplished by different persons in different offices. Thus, a single individual is responsible for producing and controlling production, for preparing the tools, supervising maintenance and repairs assigning tasks, and improving technology. As a consequence, conflicts of competence and in the assignment of responsibility are frequent. This does not improve the quality of production and its efficiency. At the same time, it is hard to conceive that the boss, supervisor or foreman of the good old days, may have time enough to dedicate himself to one of the main functions he must accomplish: to train the personnel entrusted to him.

In Italy the apprenticeship of young workers is regulated by law. The roots of the apprenticeship institution are embedded in the Middle Ages when the artisan in his shop trained young men and taught them the secrets of the trade.

According to the present Italian law on apprenticeship, our companies are authorized to hire, with reduced salaries, some young men to be entrusted to older highly qualified manual workers. These older workers are supposed to train the younger ones in the techniques acquired during many years of personal experience. In reality, nobody seems to worry whether the older worker, even if able and expert himself, knows how to teach if he wants to teach. He is justified in not being very satisfied with the idea of transmitting his skills to a possible future competitor whom the boss may prefer some day. On the other hand, most of the workers, despite their qualifications, do not have teaching skills, nor are they well acquainted with the most efficient and rapid methods of training and instructing young men. At best, the teacher will transmit only unsophisticated and rough notions, not an elaboration and an implementation of the results of his experience. The influence on the apprentice will be modest. The Italian law prescribes that, during two or three years of apprenticeship, these young men may integrate their manual training with some theoretical lessons, occupying three hours per week. But as there is no connection at all between practical and theoretical training, the efficiency of the entire process is quite low; there is to be found a large dispersion and waste of efforts.

At a higher level—foremen, supervisors, middle-managers, and managers—training and developing men's capabilities go through a process that is analogous to that of the apprentices. Of course, one must bear in mind that, in this case, apprentices generally have a secondary level of scholastic education. The training they go through is not ruled by law, but it mainly relies on the traditional habits developed in many industrial companies, in banks, in insurance companies, in many administration offices, in specialized professional centres. Presumably, even in these cases the objections raised with regard to apprenticeship of manual workers maintain their validity, notwithstanding the higher cultural level of both trainers and trainees. It is a common experience that many executives do not know what to do and how to utilize incoming assistants; they do not succeed, in many cases, in training them properly Although the executive has requested them to relieve his burden, he often complains that teaching adds a supplementary burden to his previous one.

Also, the executive at this level may be handicapped by an unmentioned and undeclared anxiety that he may be supplanted by his subordinate-trainee. Therefore, the supervisor can not be considered, in many circumstances, a good teacher and trainer unless he himself has been properly trained, directly or indirectly, in appropriate teaching methods. We must admit, on the other hand, that some supervisors may be naturally endowed or may casually become excellent trainers.

## TRADITIONAL METHODS OF INSTRUCTION

A recent survey by the National Science Foundation ('Continuing Education for R & D Careers,' National Science Foundation—NSF—69—20, 1965) indicated that supervisors influence the development of their subordinates in one of the following ways: they can exercise a stimulating action, or they may prefer not to commit themselves, or they may completely hinder their educational activities.

The study was based mainly on R & D personnel, but it is valid also for supervisors connected with production departments. This type of documentation is not available in reference to the Italian situation in industry. The scarcity of statistical data in our country does not allow of comparison with American industry.

The National Science Foundation Survey reported that from the subordinates point of view, 61% of the scientists and 49% of the engineers indicated that their supervisors stimulated and assisted them in keeping up to date. About one-third of the scientists and just under half of the engineers said that their supervisors took a noncommital viewpoint towards continuing education. Only a few reported active discouragement by their supervisors.

Those who report their supervisors as noncommittal give as an explanation of their attitude concern of the loss of their productive work time.

Previous research conducted at the Pennsylvania State University on engineers and managers reported that more than half of the supervisors were noncommittal towards their subordinates' professional development. 'Therefore, managers and supervisors, if they carry out their professional responsibilities, have as one of their prime functions the development of their subordinates. Yet few supervisors seem to be trained in this capacity.[2]

In many Italian companies, notwithstanding their elementary level of organization, however, there are to be found supervisors endowed with native capabilities and sincerely eager to educate their subordinates. Should the type of organization and the quality of the administration of these companies be higher, such capabilities would be used and promoted through suitable initiative by top managers. It is very unusual for managers to take such initiatives in our country.

---

[2] Dubin, Samuel S., Marlow, H. LeRoy, 'A Survey of Continuing Professional Education for Engineers in Pennsylvania,' Continuing Education The Pennsylvania State University, 1965.

Some Italian firms have organized and developed their own schools, primarily for fulfilling their needs for qualified manpower. In great part, it has been a question of supplementing public education. Almost all the scholastic institutions in Italy are controlled by the Ministry of Public Instruction. Only a few of them, mainly the vocational schools, are supervised and financed by the Ministry of Labour.

The schools operated by industry are not very different, in programs and methods, from the public ones except that pupils pass directly from their school desks to the factories. The difficulties they need in this crossing, when they face abruptly the differences between theory and practice, are quite similar in both types of school.

The gap between industry problems and pedagogical problems is not easy to bridge since men of the production world and men of the scholastic world communicate differently, they can not dialogue, they do not understand each other well.

The kind of instruction given in our public schools must obviously maintain a certain degree of generality and flexibility, so that pupils may face the opportunities they find in their real life, especially at the first job offered them. The internal school of an industrial firm can ignore this requirement; it can limit the field of instruction to the very specialized sector which interests the firm. The guaranteed employment that the latter furnishes probably does not compensate for the disadvantages to the young men who end up being excessively tied to the same company and its fortune. Thus they will be deprived of the possibility of transferring to other firms where their specialization would be little appreciated. On the other hand, techniques learned in public schools— manual or not manual—undergo a rapid obsolescence in the face of technological progress; and the schools, tied to a rigid governmental program generally change very slowly in respect to syllabuses, instrumentation, and methods of orienting in keeping with technical requirements. The advantage offered by internal or in-plant schools— that they are obviously more sensitive to technological changes—is offset by their narrow technical specialization and by a slow turnover of manpower. Turnover constitutes, especially in small companies, a powerful instrument for dissemination of new techniques.

Scholastic education, however, even a satisfactory one from the technical point of view, does not substantially foster the overall maturation of young men. An example which illustrates this point is drawn from the school of a large modern Italian industry. Every year this school recruited and selected its pupils from among the most brilliant young men of the area in which the firm was located in order to send them to its internal school. One particular year, the firm's request for qualifed personnel having been greater than the school output, the personnel office directed itself to a segment of young men who had been rejected in previous years. Of course, in the meantime they had been employed in other minor companies by craftsmen, in gas stations, in small maintenance and repair-shops. The manual qualification of these workers was by far lower than that of their comrades who had had the benefit of regular courses in the company's school. But the personnel department was surprised to note that their general maturation, their spirit of initiative, their capacity of observation, their ability to disentangle themselves and to manage to get along, had been developed more conspicuously than in the workers of the same age employed in well-organized factories. The handicap of an insufficient manual training was easily compensated, by means of short intensive courses.

Many deductions can be drawn from this experience. First, it calls in question traditional methods of instruction. The traditional school's aims are mainly to provide students with ideas and knowledge. In consequence, the student's capacity to think for himself, autonomously, to develop his personality is stunted; they easily become conformist. Also, the example brings into focus the efficiency of work as an agent of education. It is certain that young men discarded by the big modern firms, by working in small companies and workshops, gained valuable experience, perhaps not so much because their supervisors knew how to teach them the fundamentals of the trade, but because they had been left free to learn by trial and error. The trial-and-error method is probably costly for the firm and for the economy in general—difficult as it may be to ascertain the cost—but certainly it is of prime importance for the complete education of the individual, for his training, and for his most effective self-realization.

The value of the trial-and-error method has been discussed with regard to managers and industrialists. However, we should consider the amount of waste it involves and study the possibility of reducing the wastage. The wastage can be regarded from two points of view. On the one hand, the trial-and-error method allows for very big errors with grave consequences to the firm, eventually inviting intervention by supervisors—too late and irrational—which diminishes the educational efficacy of random experiences. On the other hand, only individuals with special natural talents, with the capability to turn to their advantage the results of mistakes, are able to profit by experience acquired by the trial-and-error method, and to utilize it later on.

## A PROPOSED EDUCATIONAL MODEL FOR INDUSTRY

While these concepts are well known everywhere, in Italy we are starting just now to take them into account and to become conscious of their complexity and to realize the mutual relationship between formal education and labour. The man on the street, young students and their parents, are mostly convinced that the links between culture and work are weak and unrelated. With regard to a future career, the scholastic diploma is considered important not for its educational value but as a symbol of social prestige and as a right to obtain privileges, in particular, to get positions in the government administration and therefore to become irremovable from the job for all life.

Of course, many persons will reach maturity with age and understand the importance of culture on the quality of their work. At their own expense they will learn how their practical experience can be enlightened by theoretical and somewhat more abstract concepts learned at school, how these concepts can assist and guide them to further experiences, and how they can frame their results within general schemes, from which they will become able to start anew and contribute to the field of general knowledge.

However, the environment of most industrial companies in our country is not conducive to promoting such a process in the individual. Continuing education is carried on in a sporadic, casual way, where only individuals who are particularly intelligent, strong and persevering will succeed. Therefore the waste of human resources, of not especially talented individuals, is very high. Having made this statement, one cannot underrate some tendencies which, once again more or less spontaneously, can be ascertained in some Italian companies. One of the most important factors towards the improving of the cultural level and especially the updating of the pre-existing notions of workers at any level, is derived from the introduction into the factories of new machinery, from the installation of new plants, from the adoption of new productive processes and techniques. Imported technologies require that the technicians learn how to use them, how to institute suitable controls and inspection systems, how to provide for maintenance and repair. Thus, further autonomous technological improvements are stimulated, the existing organizational structures are improved, and the theoretical principles on which are based the introduced technical innovations begin to be assimilated by the staff. In modern firms the innovating process is continuous. Scientific research, even if not so much advanced and widespread as in other countries, accelerates the rhythm of innovation in some of our companies, Consequently personnel at each step of the hierarchy—managers, middle-managers, and workers—are stimulated to improve individual performance.

Perhaps there is in Italy a generally diffused lack of systematic planning capacity, a reluctance to prepare programs in time and to stay with them. The *coup de main* technique—that is to say the ability to manage oneself at the last minute to solve difficult situations by inventive ability—is still highly appreciated in our industrial world. The result, however, of this type of attitude seems to be contrary to modern rational principles of education. In fact, it tends to perpetuate the pre-eminent importance of an authoritarian mentality since it exalts brilliant natural endowments of few exceptional men while it depresses and discourages the majority of individuals with average intelligence. Complaints against 'chain work,' production line work, or work 'en miettes'—exaggerated subdivision of labour into elementary manual movements—are universal. However, manufacturing and assembling times are reduced, and the advantage of resultant reduced costs cannot be underestimated. On the other side, the depersonalization of the worker resulting as a consequence of his lack of comprehension and justification of the job he is performing, is widely censured by psychologists, sociologists and writers. They have denounced the ominous dangers of alienation of the individual as a determining cause for rising tensions and dangerous trauma in the industrial environment.

However, superficial generalizations on this subject should not be emphasized. The workers to be employed in elementary operations on the line generally have a very low level of skills; they come from rough agricultural or menial jobs, the nature of which is still more depressing and unsatisfactory than the standardized work to be performed in the modern semi-automated factory. The factory environment is richer in stimuli, more stimulating mentally for the contacts it provides than rural men find working in the fields or many women experience in lonely domestic activities. Isolation and lack of human contacts, are more depressing and unsatisfying than the workshop environment, where communications and mutual relationships are a continuous source of self-education and of modest intellectual improvement. The updating influence of peers is even more intensive and important than that of supervisors. Perhaps this influence is stronger in a general education than in a specific professional one, but its consequences on the individual, even in performing his job better, may be of great value.

Successful experiments in job enlargement in some big factories have demonstrated that elementary bits of operation, very short phases, can be regrouped. It is even possible to entrust a single worker with several tasks—production operation, its checking, setting up of machines and tools, their maintenance and repair—which until now have been rigorously separated according to the criteria of specialization. Not only does alienation disappear gradually, but the advantages in quality and in cost have been assessed. However, bringing back to the job its dignity through its unity requires an improved awareness of the worker which can be reached through a better and more adequate education. For an improved training in the factories we are indebted to many subtle methods. A modern workshop technology is continually changing and impro-ving. Until now, research and project operators, the workers engaged in preparing new machineries, new tools, new jigs, in devising new processes, according to the specialization principles, have been completely separated from those who would have been entrusted with new machineries and tools, as soon as everything is set up and put in good operating order. Non-qualified workers coming in at this phase, initially react negatively, not so much for lack of training, but much more for natural psychological resistance of the individual to every abrupt innovation. Many misunderstandings could be prevented by an early participation of the unqualified or semi-qualified workers in the creative phase, when the process is in the innovative stage and research and experimantation are still going on.

A participation at each level of the company in the activities which form its objectives requires, however, intense reciprocal information, or feedback, and a broad continuous communication. An archaic conception of management imposes a formal rigid discipline and a stern silence upon the workers, the duty to concentrate on a specific allotted task, transforming the workers into robots who act according to mechanical reflexes. However, in order that the workshop does not transform itself into a chaos for a disorderly overlapping and for uncoordinated initiatives, the task of management becomes much heavier, and the management's educational component greater and more difficult. Each step must be studied; simple, clear and well defined procedures must be set up; each detail of a complex operation essentially educational must be assessed, scheduled, organized and executed with great care and sense of responsibility.

It seems evident that internal educational activities in the company do not have anything in common with the methodologies used in schools, both public or private, with their lessons, conferences, theoretical and practical exercises, examinations. Education on the job—we prefer this term to *instruction* or *training*—implies that all or most of the company's personnel must participate in the process. Everyone, in such a process, is supposed to change his role continuously, from trainer to trainee. Nor is it possible to define proper and unique didactic techniques or methodologies which are universally valid. In each company and in each special job, it is necessary to adapt—to innovate. Rather than pursuing a precise plan, the top managers must rely on a special mental attitude impressed on the personnel. An appropriate action is particularly important on the part of managers, middle-managers, supervisors and foremen.

Such a conception of the company as a source of a new kind of educational activity requires the assistance of the ordinary school. Pedagogical principles and elements of psychology should be taught in secondary schools in order that everybody may become familiar at an early age with some of their basic concepts. It is also recommended that the art of communicating, both orally or in writing, should be rapidly and significantly improved and developed in the schools of our country. Schools in Italy, the mother country of humanities, do not develop the ability of youngsters to enrich their language and to use it as a means for expressing themselves clearly, in order to reflect the more delicate shades of their thought. It is a common experience to remark in international or foreign encounters that the Italians are noticeably isolated not only for their widespread ignorance of foreign languages— Anglo-Saxons suffer of the same evil, but they can afford it—but also because they generally express themselves and communicate in an inexact, disorderly and confused way. The contrast with the French, who excel at their ability to express themselves clearly, soberly and precisely, is striking.

## CONCLUSION

I do not know whether or to what extent my critical exposition can contribute to fighting professional obsolescence, a danger increasingly acute in relation to the rapid pace of technical and scientific progress. However, an awareness of existing backward situations may enable one to realize the difficulties which are still to be overcome. It is easy to state principles, to expound quite convincing theories, but these cannot always be applied and become operative as in other environments.

In promoting advanced ideas and in trying to apply them, we often fail to assess the nature of the material—the existing human resources with and on which we have to operate. We fail to explore in advance the nature of the environment where we have to act. When that is the case, remarkable delusions will be suffered in transferring brilliant ideas and principles from one area to another having a different background.

It is in this sense that I suggest that a call to reality, which is not always sparkling as it appears on the surface—at least in my country, but, I fear, even in many others—can bring a contribution to the assessment of the objectives of this symposium.

# Factors in the Organization Climate Which Stimulate Innovation in Professional Knowledge and Skills

Pjotr Hesseling    Netherlands Economics University, Rotterdam
and Philips Company, Eindhoven

There is evidence that professional obsolescence is a serious problem. The objective of my paper is: a) to answer the question whether organizations need to prevent professional obsolescence; b) if so, to suggest how organizations can provide the means to stimulate innovation of knowledge and skills; c) to present a design of a future ideal organization which enables and stimulates participants to be leading innovators in knowledge and skill; and d) to describe action programs that change organizations towards an innovative climate.

## ALTERNATIVES TO PROFESSIONAL UPDATING WITHIN ORGANIZATIONS

When policy makers of an organization discover that the knowledge and skills of their professional employees are no longer adequate to develop, produce and offer products or services that compete with their competitors within a common area, four alternative actions seem possible:

1. They can offer considerably higher salaries for comparable jobs to attract professionals with the best level of education and skills from competitors. In this alternative, they exploit the labour environment.
2. They can restrict their industrial activities to the maintenace of profitable products or services and build a new organization with new adequate people for the new products or services. In this alternative, participants of the existing organizations are condemned to live with the older technologies.
3. They can select the more capable and younger professionals from the organization and offer them opportunities for incareer education and training. After the training programmes they can build a new unit (product division, department, plant or branch) with the successful trainees.
4. They can start with offering education and training programmes open to all participants and to move the whole organization towards a more up-to-date level of professional knowledge and skill.

In order to anticipate the implications of the four alternatives we need first to define the problem in more detail. The statement by the policy makers that knowledge and skills of professional workers is inadequate to meet the challenge of the future, is neither simple nor definite.

Despite the recent emphasis on the human value of organizations and on professionals within organizations (1), it is still extremely difficult to identify professionals within organizations and to assess their value for organizational performance. In fact, the indices for the value of professionals for organizational performace are very primitive, e.g. educational qualifications, age, the number of patents and published papers. It does not help very much to relate these indices to other indices, e.g., the value added during the process, to the return on capital employed or to the ratio of new products to old products. In my experience, most organization auditors and accountants have great difficulty in developing sensible conclusions on quality of professionals from available performance indicators. It is easier to consider professional education as consumption rather than as investment for the future, as expenses rather than as assets for quality.

The recent trend in comparative organization studies (2) has not given rise to simple and definite answers. In the Farmer and Richman tradition one expects a positive correlation between the level of education in a country and industrial performance. For example, in many developing countries professionals do not seem to fit adequately into organizations. A recent comparative study between an English and a similar French organization revealed a difference in age and education level that could explain a difference in success (3), but there are also examples of organizational failure because of unbalanced professional comptence.

Let us assume, however, that the policy makers of our fictitious organization have acceptable indicators that the poor quality of professional workers is the main reason for ineffectiveness and that they have some partial figures on professional performance (e.g. evaluation by professional associations and universities) related to organizational performace (e.g. failure in new technologies). Let us assume also that the policy makers in our example have an acceptable operational definition of professional workers, e.g. all non-routine workers who finished a long (two years or more) special training and education after general education, and who possess an accepted diploma that gives access to professional associations. Let us assume that managers who do not work within a professional area but coordinate many operations and professions, are excluded.

How can we now anticipate the implications of the four alternatives? The first alternative of overpaying seems to be only acceptable when the organizational objectives are maximization of immediate profit. Such an alternative might destroy the regional labour market and therefore the image of the organization. In European countries and especially in Japan, with a strong emphasis on loyalty and life-long pension schemes, a climate of professional labour as a commodity only is created. Employers might expect for the future hard bargaining, strikes and labour turnover, if they cannot maintain higher salaries. The organizational climate tends to be individualistic.

The second alternative of streamlining the existent organization and of building a separate unit for the future implies a risk of a conflict between the two parts. Of course, in any large and complex organization one can identify various climates and styles of management and there is some evidence (4) that people continue their favoured traditional way of working even if the environment changes. However, it seems unfair to isolate successful professional workers from new developments. It is sometimes tragic to see professional workers, because of their excellent performance in an old technology, excluded from more challenging tasks. In an unpublished comparative study between two quality laboratories, one in an established field and the other in the successive new field, we discovered a very different climate: the older technology attracted or created professionals with a more mechanistic and closed-system style and the new technology attracted or created professionals with a more organic and open-system style. The new technology laboratory showed more conflicts and attracted younger professionals. The climate between the two was different in every aspect.

It is commonplace to observe a more rapid succession of technologies, such as from electronic tubes towards transistors, linear integrated circuits, digital integrated circuits and large scale integration. If scientists and engineers need to keep pace with the technological innovation, it means that they have to be retrained every 5 to 10 years. However, the older technology is rarely completeely substituted by the newer one. In fact, forecasting tends to underrate the speed of change but also the parallel maintenance and improvement of older technologies. This implies that there is a need for parallel development of professionals: one of changing the professional orientation from innovation towards improvement, maintenance and reproduction, and another of retraining the professional for the new technology.

If the policy makers who decide to accept the second alternative, make a definite dividing line between professionals of the traditional organization and new professionals of the new organization, they will lose the best professionals and create a climate of distrust and insecurity for the future.

The third alternative of selecting the younger and more capable professionals for in-career training and as members of a new unit, seems to be very attractive. This alternative allows a more restricted effort and promises a higher pay-off in relation to the fourth alternative. Moreover, it implies the existence of fair and objective selection criteria. If the selection is open to younger professionals only, up to the age of 35, the new unit will possess an over-representation of the younger age categories and create a very competitive climate between peers.

I have had the opportunity to cooperate with older, retired consultants and I have great admiration for the mature contribution of older colleagues who are without bias or personal interests. Also Japanese organizations show examples of a better utilization of older professionals. Of course, even professionals who graduated less than 20 years ago could not pass the preliminary examinations of 1970's undergraduates, if they had to rely on the 1950's knowledge only. But experience and maturity compensate for the most recent knowledge. The present priority given to youth and younger adults needs to be balanced, in my opinion, with a fuller participation of older, even retired professionals who are ready to understand the changes. This is not a plea for a gerontocracy.

There is little clear evidence whether or how abilities deteriorate with age (5). Vernon suggests 'that in western society, adults continue to grow intellectually to 20, 30, 50 or more so long as they retain curiosity and aspire to conquer new worlds; but once they accept a mode of life and "settle down", deterioration begins.'

As long as fair and objective criteria for measuring capacity, potential and readiness for change, including maturity, are lacking, the third alternative seems to offer an unjustified advantage for younger professionals and might create an unbalanced technocracy in the new unit.

The last alternative of starting education and training programmes open to all members of an organization is very expensive. An addition of 2% to personnel costs seems to be a minimum, but for highly qualified manpower in fields of advanced technology a percentage of 7% to 10% might be needed. *Technology* is used here in a broad sense viz., the systematic application of knowledge to practical purposes. Moreover, there is here a serious problem of scale. If an organization must rely on traditional methods of transmitting knowledge via teacher-oriented lectures there will be practical limitations to such an effort. This last alternative is realistic only if we can design and develop organizations in which professional members are alternately teacher and learner and in which intrinsic motivation to innovate is fostered. Moreover, environment and market must make a future pay-off of innovation probable and the change must not prevent the maintenance of on-going activities.

## ORGANIZATIONAL MEANS OF INNOVATION

Innovation is an elusive term. Dictionary definitions do not help very much: e.g., the act of introducing anything new or different, be it methods or novelties. I define *innovation* as the conceptualisation, development and introduction of new methods, tools, techniques; of new approaches, philosophy, way of thinking; of new themes and fields of application. Examples of methods are: a new accounting system, televideo-recording of multinational meetings. Examples of new approaches are: management by objectives or matrix management. New themes are topics such as milieu hygiene, participation and well-being. New fields of use are, for example, the application of astrophysics to organization theory, or resource management to hospital administration.

Innovation implies a contrast to old established methods, approaches, themes and fields of application. The distinction between old and new can be made more easily in the cognitive field, although even there information from the past is lost because of the lack of an open and universal codification system. In the field of attitudes and feelings, however, the distinction between old and new is a matter of opinion and sometimes of labels. Even in the cognitive field innovation requires a risk-taking, entrepreneurial attitude.

The present controversy between Bruner's assumedly cognitive approach to education and continuous growth and Jones' psychodynamic interpretation of human development makes the distinction between old and new also a question of emotional maturity (6). Applied to professional obsolescence within organizations it means that organizations must create a challenging environment for inquisitive and speculative members who feel themselves deeply rooted in the organizational reality.

A study of institutionalized means of innovation for professional members within organizations suggest the following:

1. Offering a bonus and promotion to members who take part in advanced courses, deliver papers for professional associations, and to members who are officials of professional bodies. Sometimes there exist official rankings of each professional external performance.
2. Paying professional members to participate in seminars and conferences.
3. Building information review and retrieval systems within an organization. Such a network consists usually of the most respectable journals in a field and other recent publications. Members are supposed to read and review relevant papers. The rank on the mailing list tends to reflect seniority.
4. Designing career patterns with regular intermittent courses and seminars adapted

to various types and age categories of professionals. Each course provides a threshold for the next promotion. The system is sometimes called the carousel.
5. Establishing sabbatical leaves for particularly successful professionals in the form of educational travelling or of special missions.

These institutionalized forms of innovation are attractive because they can be planned and can be implemented in any large scale organization. There is a fair chance that the level of professional knowledge and skill will be up to date in an organization that has adopted some or all of these organizational rules. However, institutionalizing seems to contradict innovation. It might become an organizational mould: members conform to the rules for external reasons; there is a self-perpetuating system of so-called 'innovative' acts and rewards; participation in courses and seminars becomes a status symbol; there might be many external signals of individualistic advanced performace but members are careful not to expose themselves to risks or unfamiliar ways of thinking or acting. Organizational means of innovation are not so simple, although the five described rules might be applied with discretion.

An open climate for innovation might be reflected in the following patterns of behaviour:
—Undertaking continuous studies for the purpose of comparing professional performace with similar external groups. If possible, this should be done by outside researchers.
—Allowing informal task groups to cooperate with members throughout the organization and with external institutes such as universities and research associations. A task group might take the form of a clearing house for certain problem areas or of reading and discussion clubs. The policy makers must be open to unusual proposals recommended by task groups and even participate, on request. If necessary, special budgets must be available, e.g., for feasibility studies or informal exchange seminars.
—Supporting gatekeeper's functions within the organization. T. J. Allen of the Massachusetts Institute of Technology presented a paper recently before the Operations Research Society's Conference in London, in which he gave evidence concerning the importance of gatekeepers for R & D projects (7).
—Building open communication networks between professionals throughout the organization and outside the organization within the limits of confidentiality. This could include accessible telephone and intercom systems supported with flexowriters, telecopying devices, computer links and videophones. Continuous studies must indicate what type of communication links will be needed.
—Creating favourable conditions for exchange programmes between professionals, within the organizations (job rotation), and outside the organization (visiting appointments; extraordinary, part-time positions as researcher or lecturer). For older professionals most European pension schemes prevent even temporary mobility unless continuation of pension rights is guaranteed.
—Showing openness to unfamiliar proposals and experiments especially if suggested by junior professionals. Certain selection committees might be appointed to prevent chaotic discussions, but a final right to bring forward unfamiliar suggestions at the policy-making level seems to guarantee the best chances for innovation.
—Holding informal bar meetings open to all professionals, where top executive also will be present.

When organizations show these patterns of behaviour and have capable and resourceful education and training officers throughout the organization supported by senior line management, career patterns of professionals might be flexible and reflect continuous growth in various directions. At critical points in the career, professionals might select maintenance or management functions or continue a specialist career. The decision lies in the hands of the members, although there will be situations in which the organization must suggest alternative routes outside the organization. *However, the definition of innovation especially in professional organizations in which R & D is the main mission, defies already known solutions. Concepts of the past are not likely to be the carriers for the future.* Relevant innovations for the future certainly must comprise such concepts as open network theories of organizations with coalitions and task forces, learning conditions for a work environment, permanent education and extension work of learning centres, project education, self-development, and role reversal between teacher and student throughout the whole career. The implementation of these concepts, however, might be in unexpected directions. (8)

## FUTURE ORGANIZATIONS FOR INNOVATION: BEYOND MANAGEMENT TOOLS

It is my conviction that future organizations which enable and stimulate some members to be leading innovators in their field will escape traditional rules of control and coordination. Fantasy and creativity within open communication networks will engender conflicts and uncertainty between maintenance and innovation roles. Boundaries of traditional disciplines and professional departments will be crossed and new working coalitions emerge. However, the impact of successful innovations and the risk of unsuccessful ones are so far-reaching that new organization forms are needed to cope with innovation.

Two conditions must be met:

1. Experimental freedom must be created for testing out new concepts and ideas within given limits of resources. This does not include only a laboratory for fundamental research in the physical sciences but also fundamental research for the behavioural sciences and combinations between the two. Alternative societal developments and their possible implications for organizational patterns might be conceptualized and tested, experiments with different patterns of participation and power distribution could be carried out, new types of learning and behaviour under unfamiliar conditions could be tested and behavioural implications of new technologies might be forecast. The social responsibility of such experiments is even more overwhelming then technological forecasting suggest. The responsibility must be shared, in my opinion, with representatives of the work council and public authority. A major task is to prevent an Orwellian anti-utopian nightmare by develping behavioural and social guarantees for work organizations which are open to the values of the new generation. This type of socio-technical research needs some guarantee for the unavoidable failures.

2. On the other hand, such experimental freedom must not be completely isolated from the developments in the rest of the organization. The danger of an ivory tower, a shelter from the harsh realities of life, must be avoided. Many alternative concepts of organization emerge at the shop floor. Participant studies in such settings as the 'clean rooms' of advanced technology at the shop floor level might be a complementary preparation for members of an experimental task force. It seems necessary to bring active members from front positions into task forces and stimulate more communication and feed-back during the experiments than is customary in the physical laboratories.

## UNIT FOR STRATEGIC STUDIES (U.S.S.)

The future organization that will lead in innovation, will, in my speculation, not possess a department of socio-technical innovation or a training department in charge of these experiments. The most promising organizational developments seem to me the creation of a unit for strategic studies. Such a unit for strategic studies (U.S.S.) will not follow the normal departmental boundary lines, but consist of gatekeepers in other key departments, such as R & D, personnel and training, organization and management services, accounting, forecasting, marketing, manpower planning and information systems or whatever labels are in use in large complex organizations.
The responsibilities of a (U.S.S.) will include:
  — deciding on key issues for systematic experimentation;
  — establishing research coalitions for these issues and leasing the best available professionals within or outside the existent organization;
  — allocating resources within given limits and steering task forces;
  — forcasting the needs for the next generation of products, services and people;
  — evaluating innovative project teams and, within limits of confidentiality, similar teams in other organizations;
  — deciding on strategic organizational indices such as introducing a new type of professional — political scientists, psychiatrists — percentage of graduates, age of retirement, number of levels, type of in-career education, and nature of the organizational mission.

The chairman of a U.S.S. will be, in this speculative model, the potential successor of the chief executive officer, or chairman of the executive board. Presumably, such a unit would become operative in large, complex, multi-national corporations. This implies that new ideas will arise from the confrontation between various cultural traditions and that members have a multi-national value-orientation. Cross-cultural comparisons, not only for current performace but also for organizational forecasting, might be an essential feature of the U.S.S. Cross-cultural research provides the chance of 'shaking hypotheses free from particular sets of cultural entaglements and for catching strategic variables in new ranges' (9).

The future organization which is a leader in innovation, will, in my view, be very balanced and mature. It will not be predominantly manned with 35 year old professionals, but it will be open for guidance also by older, even retired professionals. I cannot imagine that the present trend to exclude all older people from influencing work organizations will be beneficial for a balanced growth. It is curious that professional members tend to be retired earlier than blue-collar workers whose retardation is greater. The problem of retired and idle professionals will be as serious as the introduction of the new generation.

I expect that future leading organizations for innovation will show most of the behaviour patterns as described in the previous section on organizational means of innovation. They will be more likely to spend 10% of personnel costs for updating all members of the organization than the 2% spent by progressive firms at present. There will be a more open cooperation and coalition between different types of leading organizations. If successful, the few will set the pace for the many subcontractors, entrepreneurs and independent research agencies. In the future there will be a bimodal distribution of organizations, according to my expectations: a few hundred giant concerns that can afford long-term R & D for products, services and knowledge on the one hand and numerous professional entrepreneurs, subcontractors and think tanks at the other hand.

## ACTION PROGRAMMES FOR INNOVATION

Since Bennis, Benne and Chin wrote their *Planning of Change in 1962* (10), there have been many parallel and slightly alternative routes for change programmes. The essential feature of any change programme seems to be that a deliberate attempt is made at the outset to link the various stages and levels and to think carefully through the implications of any new step. It is more important to ensure that elements of any action programme for innovation are not fragmented and disconnected. There is a readiness to accept less perfection in any special field if feedback processes allow for more interdependence of its elements. The limitations for rationality in action programmes for innovations must be accepted (11).

In my *Strategy of Evaluation Research* (1966) I tried to strike the balance between overall uniformity and individualised flexibility, between organizational structure and its functioning, between scientific rigour and pragmatic improvisation. The reactions were stimulating (12). I have recently tried to stress the importance of strategies or a meta-method to cope with the complexity of change programmes. My argument starts with an inventory of the problem areas. The stages comprise:

1. collecting information on the current use of manpower within organizations
2. selecting targets for the human potential
3. selecting means to develop the human potential with the probability of pay-off
4. selecting means to control and measure the process of change and terminal behaviour
5. measuring the net increase of human capacities as utilized in work organizations

The levels of measuring change programmes can be distinguished as:

1. level of subjective reactions of participants (how useful, how relevant, etc.)
2. level of learning (permanent behavioural changes as a result of stimuli)
3. level of behaviour in immediate work group or role set (as team member)
4. level of professional behaviour (according to professional yardsticks)
5. level of organizational performance (according to organizational objectives)
6. regional or national level

The resultant matrix shows 30 cells each requiring special variables.

The need for a complete chain of data at all levels and stages would be prohibitive for any systematic programme of change. It is, therefore, more useful to specify the expectations of the audience or clients and work backwards to answer their questions. We can distinguish the various expectations of trainees, trainers, policy makers and scientists. It seems preferable to report separately to the various audiences.

By way of conclusion I present the need for a *clear change strategy* instead of spending the main effort on elaborate details which might prove to be of little value in the final effort. I define a change strategy as the dispersion of trainers, change agents, innovators and researchers into favourable positions so as to maximize the likelihood of obtaining set objectives. A systematic change programme, with evidence on its success or failure, could be organized along four lines:

1. integrating researchers into each training and learning centre as continuous evaluators
2. building research centres with independent missionary field researchers
3. developing reliable instruments of measurement which can be objectively applied by trainers.
4. forming task forces of trainers, consultants, researchers and participant professionals with continuous feedback of the process and its results

Despite its complexity, I think that the last mentioned strategy will be the most realistic. It will make each of the parties participants in a learning situation with changing objectives (13).

As to the design of the change programme, K. E. Thurley distinguished four possible strategies (14):

1. An *a-priori* directed change programme that is implemented from the top downwards. The objectives and performance criteria are set by the top, unilaterally or jointly after bargaining. This strategy seems to be particularly relevant in bureaucratic organizations where the need for re-education and training comes from the top. It assumes one best way for organizational change and seems to underestimate the complexities and rate of change.
2. A full-scale, step-by-step change programme follows the logical steps: analysing needs, setting objectives, designing methods, implementing the change programme, analysing the results and measuring the outcome. This is a time consuming strategy that seems to be only applicable when the rate of change is moderate. In times of increased rate of change this strategy needs to retrace the first steps frequently without implementing some change.
3. A method-based change programme starts from the assumption that a particular programme will be successful and adopts principles, such as management by objectives, managerial grid or the rational decision maker. Such a strategy seems only possible if evidence has been given that the programme is the one best way for organizational change.
4. A last strategy of change seems to be the problem-solving approach. It starts from problems as perceived by some key individuals within an organization. Specific training or change programmes might help to solve the felt problems, but instead of restricting the approach to the solution of felt problems one starts from that occasional point of entrance to systematize the change programme. It is a very complex strategy because change agents, training officers and researchers need to be flexible and will meet role conflicts.

## CONCLUSION

Studies on professional obsolescence cover mainly perceived needs of professionals (questionnaire studies), manpower planning models (axiomatic), extrapolation and forecasting of technological change, and time series of vocational interest. The need for the future will be, in my opinion, studies on the process of professional obsolescence within organizations, and in our organizational society, the impact of this process on society. Field studies are required which link models, perceptions and technological requirements with behaviour.

Such studies will be facilitated by the construction of data banks of professional qualifications and performance indicators of individuals, but the main emphasis will be on strategic planning of human resources. It is still difficult to estimate how much money is actually spent on continuing education and training within organizations, because the assumptions are unclear. It is also very difficult to estimate the organizational costs of professional obsolescence (15).

However, a huge effort must be spent on designing alternative routes to innovation and fitting together data from different sources, even if the data are crude. One solution could be to develop 'entrepreneurs of change,' (quoting Ansoff's phrase to describe his new Graduate School of Management at Vanderbilt University) (16). In this view, the focus of the new professionals is directed towards coping with organizational, environmental or social change in operational items. It seems to be as relevant to the activist as to the organization man and scientist, if careful attention is given to experimental evaluation. The recent discussion on the evaluation of change pro-grammes in the *Administrative Science Quarterly* (17) shows that we should broaden our perspectives on indicators, using as wide a variety as possible for methods, factors and cultural values. At the same time we must lose our 'do-not-look-in-the-black-box attitude . . . (and) misguided hardheaded pay-off orientation, for which all that matters is the outcome, no matter how achieved.'

It is hoped that this presentation on alterantives to professional obsolescence within organizations, organizational means of innovation, future organizations, and change programmes will stimulate an experimental process-oriented approach towards innovation.

## REFERENCES AND NOTES

1.  For the human value of organizations see e.g.: Likert, R., *The Human Organi-zation*, New York; McGraw-Hill, 1967. Brummet, R. L. and others, 'Human resource measurement—a challenge for accountants,' *The Accounting Review*, 1968, 43: 217–224.
    Caplan, E. H., 'Management accounting and the behavioural sciences,' *Management Accounting*, 1969, June: 41–45.
    Blaug, M. (ed), *Economics of education*, Middlesex: Penguin Books, 1968.

    For professionals within organizations see e.g.:
    Kornhauser, W., *Scientists in Industry*, Berkeley: University of California Press, 1962.
    Orth, Ch.D. and others, *Administering Research and Development*, London: Tavistock, 1965.
    Pelz, D. C. and Andrews, F.M., *Scientists in Organizations*, New York, Wiley, 1966.

    A recent paper provides evidence that moderate bureaucracy is not detrimental to perceived professional autonomy:
    Engel, G. V., 'Professional autonomy and bureaucratic organization,' *Adminis-trative Science'Quarterly*, 1970, 15: 12–21.

2.  There is a rapidly increasing amount of comparative organization studies. In a recent exchange seminar (23–27 March, 1970) in Eersel, Holland, initiated by the author, we tried to map current studies (forthcoming publication). A useful

overview is given in: Nath, R., 'A methodological review of cross-cultural management research,' *International Social Science Review,* 1968, 20: 35–62. Schollhammer, H., 'The comparative management theory jungle,' *Academy of Management Journal,* 1969: 81–97.

3. See Hesseling, P., 'Testing a strategy of comparative organization research' in *Comparative Administration Research Institute Series,* no. 3 (forthcoming), Kent State University, Ohio.

4. See e.g. The Sears-Roebuck organizational studies in Weinshall, Th., paper presented to the exchange seminar in Eersel (see note 2).

5. Vernon, P. E., *Intelligence and Cultural Environment,* Methuen, London, 1969, chapter XII.

6. Bruner, J. S., *Towards a Theory of Instruction,* Harvard University Press, 1966. Jones, R. M., *Fantasy and Feeling in Education,* Basic Books, 1969.

7. Gatekeepers are organization members who maintain broader contact on an informal basis with colleagues outside of the organization, and they read far more of the professional journals than does anyone else in the organization.
These gatekeepers accomplish the extremely important mission of keeping the organization in contact with the outside world. My use of the notion of gatekeepers is broader than Allen's, but it seems a useful extension. See also Allen, T. J. and Cohen, S. I., "Information flow in Research and Development Laboratories.' *Administrative Science Quarterly,* 1969. 14: 12–19.

8. A review of the use of the behavioural sciences in some 300 American firms has been made by Harold M. F. Rush: Behavioural Science; Concepts and Management, National Industrial Conference Board, New York, 1969. American emphasis seems to lie mainly on laboratory training, hygienic needs, team building and conceptualisation of new models. However, I agree with Sayles that without field research organizational studies will continue to drift away from real problems towards the problems of functional specialties. See Sayles, L. Whatever happened to management? *Business Horizons,* 13, 2, 1970, 25–34.

9. See D. R. Price-Williams (ed.), *Cross-cultural Studies,* Penguin, 1969, p.30.

10. Bennis, W. G. Benne, K. D. and Chin, R. *The Planning of Change,* New York, Holt, 1962.
O'Connell, J. J., *Managing Organizational Innovation,* Homewood, Irwin, 1968.

11. Simon's concept of bounded rationality seems to be essential. See e.g. Thompson, J. D., *Organizations in Action,* New York, McGraw-Hill, 1967.

12. Hesseling, P., *Strategy of Evaluation Research: in the field of supervisory and management training,* Netherlands; van Gorcum, 1966. Reviews in *British Journal of Industrial Relations, Ergonomics, Contemporary Psychology, Journal of Management Studies, Bulletin of the Association of Teachers of Management, Business Management and Administrative Science Quarterly* (excluding non-English journals). Also discussions with colleagues provided me with stimulating feedback.

When the publisher asked me for a second printing, I felt that the need for a complete new edition, despite the time lack and effort, was more urgent than reprinting. Also in printing obsolescence is, to my regret, a serious problem.

13. Hesseling, P., Evaluation of management training in some European countries, in *Progress of Clinical Psychology*, New York, 1970 (in press)

14. Thurley, K. E., Planned change in bureaucratic organizations, paper presented to the joint conference of O.R. and behavioural sciences, London, December, 1969.

15. Since the discussions between representatives of European countries in 1961 and 1962 (see Meigniez, R. (ed.), Evaluation of supervisory and management training methods), I have tried to answer the simple question how much money is actually spent on continuous education and training within companies. Recently the Committee of the three European Communities has made a fresh start to formulate a polyvalent, occupational training policy in the European Communities (Torino, Dec. 1969), but also there the answers were not given. There is, however, some progress.
    1. Two major documentation systems on training exist in Europe at the moment: one by I.L.O. (C.I.R.F., Geneva) and another by the Committee of the European Communities (in German, French, Italian and Dutch: Documentation pedagogique—formation professionelle—since 1969).
    2. Some large companies are now implementing data banks on job qualifications and personnel descriptions. When the data banks are in operation and contain also cost figures on continuous training and education, the next step will be to use the computer in the original sense viz. not as a calculator but as an instrument for computing complex relationships between variables.

16. See *Business Week*, April 25, 1970, 85–86; also private communication on his 'A strategic plan for the graduate school of management,' September, 1968.

17. See Donald T. Campbell's article, 'Considering the case against experimental evaluation of social innovations,' in the *Administrative Science Quarterly*, March, 1970, 110–113.

# Work and Its Satisfactions in a Technological Era: A Projected NATO Environmental Study

**N. A. B. Wilson**    **Formerly Chairman, NATO Advisory Group on Human Factors, London**

Among natural phenomena, human work is amongst the most ubiquitous and most important. As such it is open to scientific study and should be so studied. Yet until quite recently this was not done, perhaps because to some it seemed too obvious a matter and to others too difficult and confused to be rewarding. This is unfortunate because the more one reflects, the more one realises the importance of work, and attitudes to work, in the human scene. As L. S. Hearnshaw has said, the kind of technical society in which we live assumes that the great majority of people will continue throughout their lives to carry out their jobs with regularity, with competence, and with a certain devotion to duty; that some at least will be willing to undergo prolonged and exacting technical or professional training, that an increasing number will apply meticulous care and attention to the building, maintenance and control of the expensive and even dangerous apparatus of civilisation; that numerous others will devote their services to promoting the health, well-being and enjoyment of the community; to say nothing of yet others whose economic productivity must subserve their own and their colleagues' satisfactions in life.

Modern technology has brought many and obvious benefits. But despite this, there are also nagging fears that it is, on balance, a cause of deterioration, by dehumanising work. The pace accelerates, scales (including the time scale) enlarge beyond comfort, people become lost in organisation, rigidity is the order of the day, and there is a marked change from tangible work to abstract and symbolic tasks. People fear that personal, human values will be overshadowed by engineering and administrative needs. In these circumstances it is very desirable that some of the scientific method and acumen which has made technology so formidable should be applied to the theme of human work, including the impact of technology on it. Otherwise both efficiency and work satisfactions could decline quite rapidly.

There have been many empirical studies during the last half century, but there are still large gaps in our knowledge of how attitudes to work are developed, how these relate to occupational choice and performance and how exactly work satisfactions, or the reverse, relate to what are conceived as incentives or even plain good working conditions. But two broad conclusions have emerged, due to the work of a series of writers from Weber to D. C. McClelland and his associates on 'the achieving society.' First, 'attitudes to work are cultural acquisitions, bound up with social organisation, economics, education and ideology, and linked to personality structure.' Second, attitudes to work, although capable of extreme persistence, can change, sometimes quite fast and radically.

Historically, however, it would be untrue to suggest that a substantial amount of research has been devoted to work activity as a unity or to evolving a powerful theory about work and its place in human life. On the contrary, most investigations by far have been *ad hoc* enquiries, usually in pursuit óf limited economic objectives and applicable, at best, within a defined range of circumstances. Enquiries have dealt with the effects of such features of the work environment as daily travel, heating, lighting, ventilation, noise, cleanliness, toxicities, bench layout, equipment, seating, etc. Since the early days of F. W. Taylor and his *Principles of Scientific Management* there has been concern with work methods and with what would now be called ergonomic adaptation of tasks and machinery. Some most useful research was done in the 1930's on monotony and repetitiveness in work and its interaction with personal and other situational variables (cf. the reports of Wyatt and his co-workers), most of which either has been or could be applied with profit today. An enormous amount of attention has been devoted to the assessment of abilities, skills and aptitudes and, to a less degree, the personal qualities and interests of operatives, foremen and managers in industry. In principle, at any rate, most researchers have taken such items as independent variables and sought to relate them to some measure of proficiency in work as the dependent variable.

Results have been, on the whole, rather disappointing for a variety of reasons. There have been fairly obvious methodological difficulties, including the fact that it is expensive and unwelcome—often to a prohibitive extent—to interrupt or modify ongoing economic processes so that satisfactory measures of this or that variable may be achieved. There is the problem of invariance: if changes suggested by a research are made, will the system work as before except for the increased proficiency envisaged? More elementarily, how stable will beneficial changes prove to be when they are founded on limited experimentation and insight and virtually no basic theory? And how do we quantify beneficial change?

To say that work of the kind mentioned above has given results which have proved disappointing on the whole is by no means to say that it has been useless. Some of it has stood up well; and at least in part as a consequence, the general standard of work environment of almost everyone today is a vast improvement on that regarded as acceptable a few decades ago. Even some of the most unpleasant and intractable environments (the dirty, the dangerous, the monotonous and inherently unrewarding) are being transformed out of recognition with the help of technology and scientific method. Many of the disappointments felt have been simply the false insights and dead ends of normal development in a new, difficult and not over-well equipped field.

Nevertheless, partly because new approaches were felt to be necessary and partly because of the development and awareness of theory in social psychology, there has been a distinct trend in the last decade or more, away from direct concern with either 'engineering' or personality variables and towards consideration of work, i.e. peoples' jobs, as fulfilling various needs; relating the degree of fulfilment of such needs to the degree of satisfaction expressed in one mode or another (e.g. by careful work, or by continuance in the position). Using a variety of methods, researchers have investigated the effects on job satisfaction of such items as the nature of the supervision or managerial style, the size and organisation of the working group, the content of the job pay, working pace and degree of autonomy, hours of work and chances of promotion. In naive terms the assumption has been that satisfaction would correlate to a usuably high degree with proficiency. But this has proved to be much too simple a view and has been replaced by working hypotheses which assume *inter alia* an interaction between personality variables and situational variables in work. Even so, the situation remains tantalizingly obscure. Vroom, whose researches and publications have been notably helpful clarifiers, points out that, at the least, we must also take account of such cultural factors as levels of expectation, the effects of reference groups, and indeed the concept of equity.

Among the most influential theories about work as a satisfier of needs have been those of Maslow and of Hertzberg. Both seem especially, though not exclusively, applicable at the level of managerial motivation, and the latter is under very active development and application in practice (not only in industry—the Canadian Defence Forces are understood to have a large, and promising, trial in progress). Maslow's theory is of the need-hierarchy type. He postulates a short series of groups of needs, i.e. disequilibria in the person, leading to responsively motivated behaviour—seeking to reduce the imbalance; and goals as the third part of the cycle, attainment eliminating the imbalance. The hierarchial concept is critical. Maslow's premise is that the behaviour of any person is dominated by the most basic of the groups of needs unfilled, e.g. physiological or safety needs will always be prepotent over needs for esteem or self-fulfilment, although these in turn may become determining when the first have been satisfied. Maslow's theory has proved enlightening, even qualitatively predictive, in fields as far apart as commerce, industry and armed forces.

But the fact remains that there is a puzzling gap between the satisfactions given by a job and proficiency at it. Intuitively, one would say there must be a substantial connection. But the correlations between them show a wide range and the median reported by Vroom is less than 0.2, which, as he remarks, has little theoretical or practical importance. A major contribution towards solving this puzzle has come in recent years from the Cornell Studies in Job Satisfaction of the team led by Patricia Cain Smith whose job description inventory is obviously a potential standard throughout industrially developed countries.

In the meantime, the crux, though not the whole, of the projected study must be to explore the possible and probable connections between satisfaction and efficiency in work. Both satisfaction and efficiency must be reckoned essential in our technologically based civilisation. To cope with the problem we must ask, in effect, to what extent there is a science of work—or obligated activity—to deal with these problems; and, in so far as it is lacking, what needs to be done to ensure the development of a science of work.